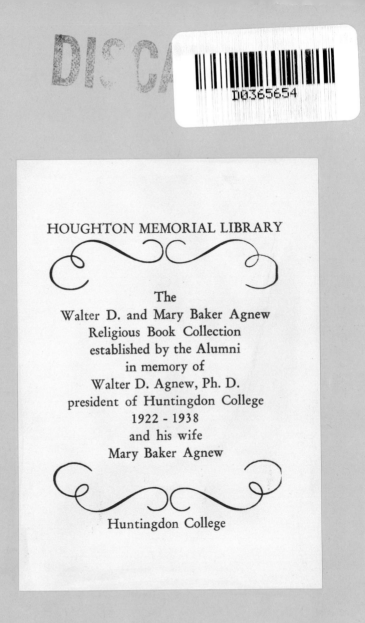

Social Justice and the Latin Churches

Social Justice
and the Latin Churches

CHURCH AND SOCIETY IN LATIN AMERICA

Translated by Jorge Lara-Braud

JOHN KNOX PRESS
Richmond, Virginia

Translated from the Spanish by Jorge Lara-Braud with permission of Iglesia y Sociedad en América Latina (ISAL), Montevideo, Uruguay.

Scripture quotations are from the *Revised Standard Version of the Bible,* copyrighted 1946 and 1952.

Contents

Introduction

This book should be no more than a summary of the discussions and reports presented at the Second Latin American Conference on Church and Society at the Presbyterian Retreat Center of El Tabo, Chile, January 12 to 21, 1966; in a certain sense it is just that. Nevertheless, at the time that the participants in the conference were to determine the character to be given this publication, there was unanimous recognition that the climate of the El Tabo meeting had reached such intensity that it could not be reconstructed simply by collecting and recapitulating its substantive components. The element of vitality, the most striking note of the conference, had created a living dialogue, often accompanied by heated discussions and fiery zeal. These features predominated in every activity as a consequence of the climate of the conference itself, in which spontaneous ideas, the set of problems before us, and the historical circumstances of those days found us deeply involved, making it impossible for us to remain unmoved, silent, or apathetically tolerant.

Unfortunately (or should we say fortunately?) there has been no systematization of that dialogue. The effect of the discussion was the immediate stimulation of dialogue and the often burdensome necessity of developing ideas once believed thought out and settled for good. As for their preservation, there was no record other than the instantaneous and therefore perishable function of the thinking process, although we know that by that process we are nourished and by its action we get at the essence of our being and doing.

To be able in some way to interpret all that the conference signified, it was resolved to attempt an unusual procedure for this report. The material collected in the present volume has indeed sprung from a compilation of the principal expositions of the different parts of the agenda and the reports of the study committees that met during the conference. But that material has been part of a later process of collecting and editing the total output, with the result that the book here offered is in a certain sense something more than the sum of the component parts of the conference: This book is an attempt to recover—through avoiding a simple mechanical collection of documents—the spirit that vitally animated the meeting at El Tabo.

In terms that intend to be objective, this book summarizes what may be considered an original contribution to Protestant thought in Latin America. The outcome is the product not of a few "thinking heads" but of the efforts of a real community of believers representing a wide variety of theological currents and nuances—a community in which the encounter and communal reality were not always experienced by intellectual agreement, but by participation in one faith and obedience to one Lord. The message and the contribution of this book should be interpreted in that context—not as the work of a group, a current of thought, or a certain theology, but as a communal effort in which are present both the tensions as well as the profound, unrecorded, and revealing insights which are reached only in the midst of a true community.

1

Huampaní and El Tabo:
Two Stages and Several Discoveries

When the Second Latin American Conference on Church and Society was convened in mid-1965, the abbreviation ISAL (Iglesia y Sociedad en América Latina) and the movement identified with it were already well-known by the Protestant community in Latin America. Four years of patient and fruitful work had made this possible. The immediate precedent, which was widely recognized, was the Conference of Huampaní (Lima, Peru, July 1961), in which for the first time Protestants from the whole continent joined together to consider specifically the meaning of Christian responsibility in the face of rapid social transformation. Until then, the phrase "Church and Society" had been used by a small group of believers, originally found in Brazil and in the Río de la Plata area, to designate that polarity considered by many as insoluble and scandalous —the concern of Christians with the social phenomenon as a thing in itself. That is to say, a concern devoid of hidden meanings or intentions, in which the evangelical attitude in its traditional orientation—winning converts— had been temporarily put aside, yielding to the urgency of a more disinterested and determined preoccupation for man. Accordingly, "Church and Society" was the formula chosen to express this new attitude: Christians concerned for society as such, for the situation of man in that society, for the socio-economic conditions that determine human frustration and suffering in a limited and concrete setting,

Latin America. It was also the formula found to express a new concept of Christian witness through service and the fulfillment of social and political responsibilities which the believer shares with every citizen.

The proposition, as has been said, could not fail to remain "scandalous" for many. How could they accept a concern which would relegate to a secondary position the evangelistic mission of the church? Would that not be disobedience to the fundamental command given by Christ to the Apostles and transmitted to believers until the end of time? Would that disobedience not mean a denial of the exclusive mission of the church and, thereby, the rationale for its being throughout history? The group that had given life to the ideas of "Church and Society" had to confront this type of questioning from the very beginning, since these issues, found in the very heart of the gospel and posited by the predominant currents in Latin American Protestantism, could not be disregarded.

In general, it may be said that attempted answers to the above and interpretations of the charisma of "Church and Society" followed, in the beginning, two principal lines of reasoning. On the one hand, precisely that term "charisma" was emphasized, indicating that "Church and Society" designated a particular ministry of the church, the field of social concern; there was, therefore, no reason to think that the evangelistic mission had been relegated to a secondary plane. It was a matter of two ministries, simultaneous and different, and in order of priority social responsibility appeared clearly subordinate to the evangelistic task.

The second line of reasoning went somewhat further. It admitted that social concern was only one specific charisma of the church but that ministry did not exclude the fundamental responsibility of the Christian nor was it to be subordinated to other presumably more basic activities of the religious community. In exercising his social responsibilities, the Christian performed his witness; his proclamation of Jesus Christ followed other methods and responded to new circumstances, but it did not therefore cease to be an essentially evangelistic task. One could speak of specific ministries with regard to the differentiation of methods and tasks, but in what concerned the ultimate end of the gospel, social concern was as valid and important a testimony to Jesus Christ as the traditional practices of evangelistic activity.

That was more or less the state of affairs reflected by that first continental meeting at Huampaní on "The Responsibility of the Protestant Church in the Face of Rapid Social Changes," which gathered forty-two delegates representing seventeen Latin American countries and fourteen different denominations. Huampaní signified a new awareness and at the same time the first important application of a method of analysis which later would be repeated with varying efficacy in the series of regional conferences which followed. The method consisted of analyzing separately the basic aspects of the Latin American reality (economic, political, socio-cultural) and then relating the most evident characteristics and needs of the situation to the church. It was a matter of establishing an initial relationship, an indispensable line of communication between the two realities expressed in the Church and Society movement. Perhaps the most important aspect of this procedure has been the confrontation, the unrestricted consideration of pragmatic matters, effected by juxtaposing these two realities. As far as one can tell, until then the Protestant church and Latin American society had remained inexplicably and intentionally oblivious to each other.

The first consequences of that unprecedented act were

observed during the course of the conference itself. There existed, of course, certain presuppositions with which the application of the method had been justified. The given presupposition of analyzing Latin American society was that the principal goal was to determine a strategy for the church, examining the spheres of secular life in which its presence and message would have special relevance, and, as the counterpart of that analysis and in accordance with the conclusions drawn from it, to put into effect not only the forms of exercising social responsibility but also the basic organization and the program of activities of church life. This attitude represented a tremendously significant change in the way of conceptualizing and studying social responsibility. Nevertheless, the nature of that change was quantitative, not qualitative. Even as the work of Huampaní was unfolding, the agreed-upon assumptions—an inhibition upon the reflections—led to what may be described paradoxically as the most important result of the conference: perplexity and frustration. The study of social realities demonstrated that the church found itself facing an overwhelming situation. The attempt had been made to analyze a process of rapid social changes of a dazzling pace and absorbing nature, but in the last analysis the conviction prevailed that it was a process of an external social order, essentially different in nature from the church. The study then proceeded to discern the transformation, which had already been dubbed the Latin American "revolution," was affecting the very core of the life and organization of the church. It was an event—and this was the discovery of Huampaní—which involved and conditioned the church. In the light of that discovery, nothing could be more mistaken than feigning an attitude of impassibility and objectivity, determining in advance what changes would be needed in the life of the church in order to adapt or modernize its strategy. The profound impetus and the sense of change were found to spring from the inner being of society, and the church was caught in the midst of the same tensions and divisions as the society in which its own body had received life and form.

This fact, whether or not sufficiently explicit, constituted in Huampaní the first awakening to the profound significance of the Latin American revolution. It was at once the inchoate and stimulating point of departure for the study and thought which would begin to be developed in the Latin American Board of Church and Society.

Church and Society in Latin America (ISAL), or the Latin American Board on Church and Society as the movement was first called, grew out of the initiative of the Huampaní Conference and was officially constituted in February, 1962, under the sponsorship of five Latin American interdenominational bodies. Its first method of procedure, afforded by the meeting at Huampaní, was to issue a substantial collection of reports and working papers under the title "Encounter and Challenge" to stimulate the creation of local and regional study groups as the bases for future expansion of the movement. In January, 1963, in Buenos Aires, the second plenary session of ISAL met and drew up a plan of studies and publications to be finished in late 1965. The structure set up for the first time there (subsequently revised and reinforced innumerable times) determined the basic course of thinking and the nature of the studies which led to the Second Latin American Conference on Church and Society.

Only by a necessary oversimplification can one establish basic landmarks in an essentially fluid and continuous process which rendered diverse tendencies and interpretations of the meaning and methods of its own mission, as usually happens in a movement that prefers the dialectical vitality of debate to doctrinal rigidity. Nevertheless, in spite of the risks of schematization, an indication of some of those possible guidelines is imperative.

Let it be remembered that Huampaní had reached an elusive discovery, a certain creative perplexity. What was the real nature of social change? Precisely what constituted the revolutionary transformation of Latin America: What were the roots from which this change operated on the social structure? Why did the church find itself involved in and conditioned by that change—inside rather than outside the revolution as had been assumed at one time? Questions of this nature, probably never explicitly formulated, led to the discovery of the basic, though not necessarily original, notions which made possible the first tentative answers.

The first idea belongs to the current socio-economic concept, that of structure. Upon it hinged the attempt at a satisfactory interpretation of the nature of social change in Latin America. That change did not consist, as might have been assumed, simply of updating the existing social, political, and economic institutions in consonance with the exigencies of a new situation. It was a change beginning to operate on the basic configuration of society, a transformation at once horizontal and vertical, beginning with a broadening and restructuring of the foundations of the Latin American social framework. Only this type of all-inclusive change, from the groundwork to the surface, could properly be called revolution. In its studies and publications ISAL used the term "revolution" more and more frequently for tacitly identifying a structural concept of change with the dynamic ingredients and profound roots of the social process.

As for the transformation of the church itself, one could not fail to note that as an institution subject to the laws of social change the church was to be found within the very process. Having its roots in the structure whose foundation was being undermined, it not only would be affected on the superficial level of its organization and institutional life but would suffer profound changes closely related to the transformation of the entire society.

At this point the necessity of another approach was realized: the discovery of a theological category that would make possible an interpretation, from the viewpoint of the church, of the nature and meaning of this profound change, the social revolution. The notion of the concept of *history* arises and is resolved in a *theology of history*. The characteristics of social change in Latin America and the global nature of the process have made necessary a sweeping reconsideration of history. Consequently, an interpretation of the present situation grounded in a comprehensive and meaningful process is indispensable. From the biblical standpoint that process is history itself—history considered not as the exclusive business of man, but principally as the deed of God, the unfolding of his will for the redemption of man, ushered in, known, and interpreted by the revelation in Jesus Christ; man thus becomes the subject and object of historical change. The "humanization" of man is the "interim telos" (Masao Takenaka) of history, the immediate and "penultimate" goal (Bonhoeffer), which anticipates the final union of all things in Jesus Christ. Beginning with this theological interpretation, Latin American social change, with its revolutionary nature and the unmistakable tenor of renewal efforts in search of social justice, would acquire new meaning for the church. No longer would the concern be confined to a specialized ministry (social responsibility) or to a concept of the revolutionary state of the continent as a simple class concern. The action of God is manifest in sociohistorical events, and the church stands not on the margin, but in the very heart of the process. Social revolution is also the revolution of the church. The impulse that transforms social structures to create new forms of human existence, conditions that give man new opportunities for "humanization," is the very impulse that directs and defines the present understanding of the mission of the church—not just one partial aspect, but her total, unique, and true mission.

To this reflection on history are added several secondary ideas that have formed part of the subject matter of ISAL. The concept of *ideology* and the idea of contemporary *secularization* were concrete aspects which had to be considered in light of a theology which saw in history the disclosure and realization of the will of God. In this context, ideology emerged as an attempt to interpret historical and social reality from within, that is, from the whole realm of secular thought amid historical change. It was not only an interpretation but a dynamic perspective for orienting the social transformation toward precise objectives. At this point, a fact of prime importance for Christians was confirmed: The type of social transformation advanced by definite Latin American ideological tendencies coincided with the central movement toward new forms of "humanization" which we Christians also saw in history. Dialogue between Christian faith and the revolutionary ideologies therefore appeared possible and necessary. Not that in the possibility of dialogue was hidden the subtle attempt to upstage secular ideological currents; rather, ideology was the natural realm of politics in actual practice, the means of arriving at commitment and action in social transformation as defined by a theological interpretation of history. This meant going beyond the false dichotomy between faith and ideology and understanding that Christian faith must itself be expressed through political ideologies or social change, even though that expression is always incomplete, imperfect, and inconstant.

In a certain sense this same reflection made possible a Christian understanding of contemporary secularization. The rise of a secular society and mentality determined a new understanding of the religious event. How then is the contemporary mission of the church, particularly of the Protestant church in Latin America, to be conceived? Have the language and forms of religious communication lost all meaning? Should we immediately assume the urgent task of finding the new language intelligible to a secular society? Was, perhaps, emphasis on the social awareness and responsibility a first response to that search? In that case, what substantial modifications of the church's forms of communal life and witness would be required? Would we not first try to get to know in depth the Latin American socio-cultural ethos before we could determine concretely the new life-forms of the Christian community?

The theme of secularization thus climaxed the process of reflection on the questions which ISAL had asked itself. With the purpose of formulating replies to this bristling set of questions, the meeting was called for January, 1966, in El Tabo, Chile.

Since this whole volume is an attempt to share the thinking of the Second Latin American Conference on Church and Society, it would be superfluous simply to summarize its findings. Nevertheless, two facts may be indicated which will help interpret the conference and its undeniable contribution to the development of Protestant thought in Latin America.

In the first place, El Tabo acted as a catalyst which promoted and gave form to the insights and incipient responses which ISAL had attempted thus far. The systematization attempted in this section would have been impossible before the conference. In the preparations, in the formulation of the agenda, and finally in the exhaustive study accomplished during the meeting, the ideas and theological statements developed by ISAL until that time were summarized, and in some cases first attempts were made to systematize them. Obviously ISAL does not mean to attribute to a certain sector in the movement nor to its permanent staff the credit for having originated a certain theological current. This current was the outcome of a different process of individual efforts (although the name of Richard Shaull should undoubtedly be singled out) to which should be added the contributions of scattered and heterogenous groups through their participation in the conferences, study groups, and institutes organized by ISAL and through their writings in the publications of the movement. ISAL thus successfully created (as demonstrated by the second conference) not only the environment propitious for an ecumenical meeting in Latin America but also a current of theological thought—perhaps the first in the history of Latin American Protestantism—related specifically to the continent and intentionally ecumenical rather than denominational.

If in one sense the conference served as catalyst for the ideas and perceptions born of study, the second effect, equally important, was of the opposite nature. El Tabo provoked theological confrontations, clashes of opposing currents, and sharp debates over problems of the interpretation and strategy of the movement. In one sense, then, the conference molded and formulated the product of an intense period in the history of ISAL; on the other hand, it unchained new reactions, brought to the surface latent disputes, and gave rise to a theological discussion surely to be expanded during the coming years (a second period of the movement). This discussion will lead to new theological syntheses and clearer perceptions of the mission of the church, the new structures of fellowship, the meaning of

Christian presence in social change, and the concurrence and integration of the Protestant community based on an authentically inspired concept of ecumenism in Latin American life.

2

The Historical Juncture

During recent years the statistics giving detailed accounts of the wretchedness in which the masses of Latin America live have become overwhelming. The statistics stand before us, prepared by responsible groups. In various conferences we have repeatedly read and studied the data and percentages, inventories of the most sordid aspects of life on this continent: hunger, illiteracy, lack of resources, infant mortality, the slim chances of the great majority for reaching an acceptable level of living. The facts have been carefully gathered and we are fully conscious of them, but being conscious of misfortune through figures is one thing; suffering and living in it quite another. Those of us in positions to analyze statistics always constitute the privileged minority excluded from the percentages cited. The only responsible answer is, therefore, to assume a form of commitment and action capable of attacking the root causes of subhuman living conditions in Latin America. That is the lesson which we Protestants of the continent, together with other groups both Christian and non-Christian, have learned in the last few years. Love of neighbor compels us to meet him in his own situation, even as the Christian ministry of service is manifest today in the struggle for a fuller humanity.

So when we speak of "Latin America today," we should begin by recalling the wretchedness which still exists here.

This chapter is based on the presentation by Leonardo Franco.

This constitutes the shadow of the other Latin America which is also real: the continent of monumental buildings, thriving industrial centers, the elite few who enjoy their exquisite customs and privileged life. But "Latin America today" is also the growing awareness of that misery and the fight already unleashed to erase it for good—a relative novelty in Latin America and the rest of the world. The great masses are becoming conscious of their situation, science is studying the causes of poverty, and the chief end of politics is—or pretends to be—the transformation of that situation. It has become clear to all that the impoverished conditions of vast sectors of humanity, the existence side by side of rich and poor, are not the result of some irremediable natural phenomenon nor of orders of creation, but are determined by man himself. Since man has been the agent of that imbalance, in him also are to be found the possibilities of overcoming it. But one learns all this only in the midst of a giddy process requiring constant analysis of the situation and efforts to conceive the means of rectification. Many Christians are caught up in this process; many of us here have come to think of this social revolution which is sweeping the continent in search of more just socio-economic structures as a challenge which we cannot ignore if we wish to be obedient to the commission of Jesus Christ.

As our proposed theme is inexhaustible, any approach will be partial and incomplete. Among the various possible options, we here choose to analyze the political situation of Latin America—that is, the form presently assumed by the struggle for political power—thus omitting an analysis of the social and cultural situation, of the basic economic problems and their causes, and of ideological alternatives. All these are indispensable aspects for orienting ourselves, but excellent material covering them already exists in various publications of ISAL. Neither does it seem necessary to stop here to justify the urgency or the need for the creation of new conditions of life and the simultaneous elimination of structures and interests that produce suffering and bring about the inexorable deterioration of personal and institutional life in our countries. This change has been named the "Latin American revolution." Our task is not to demonstrate the necessity of the revolution, but—taking that as given—to try to indicate at what point in the revolutionary process we find ourselves.

The optimism which came over many of us in the years following the Cuban revolution and which now appears to have been naive has given way to discouragement and dismay as to the path of the Latin American revolution. We have discovered by a rude awakening that the obstacles to social change in Latin America often appear hopeless for the forces fighting for that transformation. In the very heart of these forces there is bewilderment as to the plan of action, resulting in fragmentation and even the factionalism of the Latin American left.

We can designate three different but closely related aspects of this situation to interpret the import of the present moment in the revolution in which Latin America lives.

The Rigidity of Defenders of the Status Quo

In this section two facts will be considered: the attitude of the United States toward Latin American popular movements and the resurgence across the continent of militarism shielding the political actions of the minorities interested in maintaining the status quo.

Unfortunately, in the U. S. attitude toward Latin America is perhaps the chief clue to understanding our situation: the phenomenal growth of the United States since World War II and its expansion in our world. In the words of an Argentine economist,

The United States emerged in 1945 with insignificant military losses, with assets calculated at $42 billion, as the sole investment power with a vastly expanded productive capacity, surplus capital, and undisputed control of world commerce and finances, possessing military bases and imperial power in the most strategic zones of the globe. All of these advantages have continued expanding since 1945. Through the natural dynamics of this process the United States have sought to impose a hegemony over the *free world,* operating directly out of Washington and New York, and indirectly through the old imperial powers (Great Britain, France, Germany, Japan) trying to reduce them to subordinate roles. Private investments, government loans, monopolistic control of international trade and technological progress, a complex network of politico-military instruments and agreements, a worldwide ideological offensive, alliance with the ruling and middle classes of other capitalist nations and parts of the Third World—such are the principal mechanisms employed by the United States in its venture in world hegemony.[1]

U. S. intervention in Latin American affairs must be viewed, not in isolation, but in the larger context of this nation's appropriation of political, economic, and military supremacy in the modern world. But the exercise of this power in Latin America assumes a special tenor: The United States has always considered Latin America its "sphere of influence," a region which because of geographical proximity must be protected from extra-regional penetration. Following this conviction, already set forth in the Monroe Doctrine (1823), the United States assumed the right of intervention, even military intervention, in the affairs of Latin American nations. According to the account of the Mexican scholar, Jesús Silva Herzog, the number of military and diplomatic interventions comes to forty-two in the past sixty-six years. A more subtle but no less determinative force has been economic penetration and political pressure.

The Cuban revolution and subsequent social awakening among vast sectors of the Latin American populace introduced a new element into hemispheric relations coincident with the inauguration of President Kennedy and his young government team. The North American government appeared to take a new attitude toward its southern neighbors owing to a different concept of the political task which distinguished the Kennedy administration from its predecessors but also, in relation to Latin America, as the result of a fear of a social revolution alienating the rest of the continent from North American influence. The Cuban revolution was too direct a challenge to be taken lightly. Apparently grasping seriously the necessity of social changes in Latin America, the North American government adopted a new approach, trying to direct those changes so that existing relations between the two Americas would not be altered.

The Alliance for Progress plan presented by Kennedy at the inter-American meeting in Punta del Este in 1961 initiated the apparently new phase in hemispheric relations. The plan was designed to offer a capitalistic alternative for Latin American development. The idea was to put an end to decadent social structures and, through the foreign aid of the wealthy nations, to bring about in the underdeveloped countries that economic "take off" which was to transform them into prosperous capitalist societies.

After five years of a ten-year plan we confront a judgment on the effectiveness of the Alliance which is not merely partisan, but is shared even by those who were most optimistic and/or complacent about its purpose and outcome. Alberto Lleras Camargo, one of the most enthusiastic proponents of the plan, came to say that the celebration of the fourth anniversary of the Alliance for Progress was a melancholy ritual. The Latin American people heard with indifference the figures delivered in speeches and the renewed promises. Neither in official nor public circles was there any spirit of celebration.[2]

A summary record of the accomplishments of the Alliance points to construction of houses, schools, and hospitals in significant numbers, but no real change in the panorama of the needs of our people. One must recall that the commitments accepted by the Latin American governments were not satisfied; the matter of "putting our own house in order" through various reforms was not even attempted in most of the countries. The North American government, on the other hand, hardly fulfilled its part of the agreement. (The figures made available to the Latin American governments in the four years that had transpired were under the established commitment of the 200 million dollars a year promised for the ten-year period.) Still more revealing, many of the grants came as welfare measures unrelated to development, while others were handled rather dubiously by the Latin American governments. The majority, however, were loans extended to finance the purchase of North American products by Latin American governments (as in the case of the recent purchase of four Boeing airplanes by the Argentine Airlines, financed by the U. S. Bank of Exports and Imports) under the terms of the Alliance for Progress. Numerous examples of this type demonstrate how the Alliance has furthered the penetration of North American production in Latin America. The Alliance for Progress era, however, has been left behind in hemispheric relations, its goals frustrated and its original political motives cast aside.

With the death of Kennedy, the North American policy toward Latin America passed from what has been called "conservative reformism," characterized by an attitude of encouragement to liberal governments, to a new "big stick policy," manifest in the support of any type of government which plainly and clearly satisfies U. S. ideological, military, and economic interests in the hemisphere. This change played a crucial role in the revolutionary process in Latin

America. While it is quite true that Kennedy was unyielding toward any ideas or signs of Marxist inspiration, his vision of the social process was much more dynamic and conducive to understanding non-Marxist liberal movements in Latin America. In contrast, the Johnson administration was more interested in defending the status quo at any price than in spurring even the most moderate liberal reformist impulses. This new policy was converted into a categorical opposition to any popular innovative movement, regardless of ideological affiliation—a frontal opposition admitting direct intervention and military invasion. The events marking the gradual intensification of this attitude are well-known. For the record, the most important were the following: the appointment of Thomas Mann as chief advisor to Johnson on continental affairs—ex-Ambassador to Mexico, sadly known for his advocacy of a hard-line policy toward popular movements in Latin America and his subsequent declaration in 1964 amply publicized as the "Mann Doctrine," according to which the United States reserved the right of recognition of revolutionary governments in Latin America in accordance with U. S. interests; following suspiciously close to the announcement of Mann Doctrine, the Brazilian overthrow of April 1, 1964, which was calculated to halt the rapid progress of social awakening under the Quadros and Goulart administrations; the Bolivian *coup d'état,* inexplicable (according to the deposed President Paz Estenssoro) except for the policy of reorganizing the Army which the North American government imposed on Bolivia as a condition for economic aid, putting an end to the revolutionary process begun in 1952; U. S. military intervention in the Dominican Republic in the last week of April, 1965, to check the popular rebellion which sprang spontaneously from the military uprising against the existing *de facto* government and to insure thereby the preservation of the status quo in that country, as has been demonstrated in the ensuing months; the North American proposal, backed by the majority of Latin American governments, but resisted and defeated by a group of nations headed by Mexico, Chile, and Uruguay, to create a joint military force to intervene in all situations threatening the present status of the continent; the declaration by the U. S. House of Representatives on September 20, 1965, stating (although only unofficially, as in the case of the "Mann Doctrine") that any manifestations or threats of subversion in Latin America were a violation of the Monroe Doctrine and our collective security and, consequently, that it reserved the right to take steps, in self-defense through armed force, to prevent or combat intervention, domination, control and colonization in any form within the Western Hemisphere by known subversive forces, such as communism and its agents. The declaration passed by a vote of 312 to 52, and, according to *Time,* was endorsed by fifteen of the nineteen U. S. ambassadors in Latin America. It is already well-known how loosely the label "communist" or "communist agent" is applied to any movement favoring social change in Latin America.

To this list of events may be added the diplomatic maneuvers executed in two important elections in the latter half of 1964: In September in the Chilean elections the Christian Democratic candidate Eduardo Frei, although the most courageous critic of the United States within the Organization of American States, was nevertheless a more favorable alternative for North American policy than Salvador Allende, the Popular Action Front candidate. In an even clearer case, North American interests and the diplomacy of the English Colonial Office succeeded in changing the electoral system of British Guiana in order to prevent the continuation in power of leftist leader Cheddi Jagan and avoid the risk of "a second Cuba" in the hemisphere.

As the counterpart to this interventionist attitude of the United States, we find a resurgence of militarism in several Latin American nations. In some instances, armies dissatisfied with their political power in their own countries have tried to establish the means for unilateral action in neighboring nations in order to protect the ideological unity of the continent. The facts linking the Brazilian and Argentine armies, probably the two most powerful in the region, with this position are notorious. In an interview with Argentine and Brazilian military spokesmen considering the question of possible joint intervention in Uruguay, General Onganía, commander of the Argentine Army, allegedly declared that "for Latin American armies there should be no political boundaries, only ideological ones." Also quoted was the following statement from a confidential Brazilian document: "The Brazilian government regards as suitable the new principle of sovereignty based on a common political and social system, and not on obsolete physical or political boundaries."[3]

In addition, a political balance on the continent indicates a strengthening of the right in several countries by various means: either by violent overthrows (seven of the present Latin American rightist governments gained power by direct seizure: Guatemala, El Salvador, Honduras, the Dominican Republic, Brazil, and Argentina) or instead by hindering the progressive measures of constitutionally elected governments (for example, the Popular Action in Peru). In other cases, governments are conservative (Colombia and Uruguay), manage a repressive machine (Venezuela), or maintain rightist military regimes masquerading behind sham elections (Nicaragua, Paraguay, Haiti). The continent's two most serious and promising attempts at structural change, the cases of Cuba and Chile, have been left aside in this survey for the time being. We shall subsequently examine the effects of the crisis in leftist leadership on the Cuban revolutionary process; in the case of Chile it would be premature to assess the Christian Democratic Party and its stated goal of transforming socio-economic structures. Several Latin American analysts of the same political persuasion have pointed out that after one year Frei won the backing of many progressive circles in the hemisphere for his firm policy of international independence, but, at the same time, they are skeptical of the chances of renewing old social and economic structures without an open rupture with the groups which have tried for so long to preserve them. Meanwhile, Chile, Argentina, and Uruguay, formerly or up until now the three most advanced countries in capitalist terms of development, continue to show signs of economic stagnation, indicated by the slight increase in gross national product and net per capita income. The year 1965 was especially damaging for Uruguay.

Colombia, in turn, is undergoing a severe economic crisis accompanied by a devaluation of the currency in a pre-election period. The hardening of the right, on the one hand, and the rise of revolutionary and guerrilla movements, such as that sparked by the priest Camilo Torres, on the other, make Colombia one of the most explosive situations on the continent. Equally as critical and dramatic are the situations in the Dominican Republic, Ecuador, Bolivia, Brazil, and Argentina already mentioned. This is the view, only hastily sketched, of the struggle for power in Latin America today.

Consequences of the International Situation

In the years following the Second World War the world split into two ideological blocs with their respective capitals in Washington and Moscow. In addition, a third group of nations was emerging, principally from former colonial re-

gions, which maintained a policy of independence in relation to the two blocs. This group articulated its thoughts in
the conference of Afro-Asian nations convened at Bandung,
Indonesia, in 1955. At this meeting something was glimpsed
which subsequent years have confirmed: The division of
the modern world does not correspond to an ideological
confrontation in terms of communism and capitalism, but
principally to an economic phenomenon: rich nations and
poor nations.

One of the revolutionary possibilities for Latin America
lay in bolting the Western political sphere and joining the
group of nations with political autonomy. Greater obstacles
to the realization of this aspiration are constantly arising.
As time advances, the possibility of maintaining political
independence of the blocs competing for world power becomes more difficult. Let us examine some factors underlying these assumptions.

A closer analysis of North American and Soviet realities
shows us that in recent years there have been more similarities than differences in spite of the ideological chasm that
presumably separates them. Both are highly developed countries, the United States more so than the Soviet Union,
with high standards of living. The welfare of their own
people constitutes one of the main goals in the policies of
both powers. This fact was recently pointed out by a Marxist university professor: "The Soviet Union is presently more
interested in the industrial revolution than in the social
revolution." Moreover, the enormous nuclear power of both
nations constitutes a threat of potentially tragic consequences
in the event of armed conflict. This is more than sufficient
reason for both powers to play down the points of friction.
Although this is mostly a matter of conjectures based on
study of the international situation, the evidence is sufficient
to conclude that in spite of mutual accusations and griev-

ances, there is a basic agreement between the United States and the Soviet Union to "control" their disagreements. The cold war has thus reached the point of freezing.

These signs that the danger of a nuclear war has been averted, without a doubt, constitute grounds for optimism; but the question of the poor nations of the world is whether the price of this icy peace is to be the continuation of their poverty. It is well-known that the frictions which have created and may yet create international tensions arise mainly from the development needs of the peoples of the third world. An understanding between the two great powers based on recognition of their respective spheres of influence, abrogating and delegating the right of intervention in such areas to stifle revolutionary designs, without the possibility of reprisal by the other power, constitutes one of the facts that has paralyzed the social revolution in the third world. The doctrine of peaceful coexistence has thus brought the USSR and Communist Parties around the world which follow its policy to renounce the more aggressive methods of propagating the revolution, disregarding the fact that world peace at such a price means little or nothing to the poor people of the third world.

It would be premature to say that the sense of unity attained by the Afro-Asian peoples as a result of Bandung has been lost, but lately several events have greatly endangered their future. Moreover, they find themselves now unable to hold the conference which was to have met in Algeria and which might have seen the marginal nations take a new position in relation to the industrial nations. In addition to the Sino-Soviet conflict, which undermined the preparations for the conference, several of the leading "uncommitted" nations have experienced major convulsions, which put in question their ability to carry out the enormous task of directing social change in the third world. Ben Bella and Sukarno, important promoters of the Afro-Asian unity, were the leaders of coups in their respective countries, Algeria and Indonesia.   Subsequently, Ben Bella was overthrown and Algeria was left facing an uncertain future. Sukarno managed to come out of the Indonesian rebellion apparently unharmed but shaky. Newsmen led us to understand that he continued to govern subject to conditions imposed by the rightist military. At the same time, India, the largest of the uncommitted nations and erstwhile advocate of peaceful methods, resorted to war against neighboring Pakistan.

Recently the first Tri-Continental conference met in Havana, where Latin American delegates participated as full members along with the representatives of African and Asian nations. Apart from the scattered and generally biased news accounts, there is no basis for judging whether this conference has been able to consolidate the precarious unity of the African, Asian, and Latin American revolutionary movements. On the contrary, it appears that the same tensions which thwarted the conference in Algeria were again at work on this occasion.

In summary, the international situation, the effects of the policy of peaceful coexistence, and especially the crisis of the nations of the third world seem conducive to an inauspicious juncture for social revolution, whose accelerated and seemingly unbridled pace we noted with optimism a few years ago. A third element, finally, has coincided to make the present situation more complicated and unpredictable.

Crisis in the Leftist Leadership

In referring to the "crisis of the left," we are thinking chiefly of the groups of a Marxist ideological orientation. Insofar as our commitment as Christians in Latin American society has been gaining in depth and maturity, we have become increasingly aware of the importance of Marxist movements in the promotion of social change in the hemisphere. Whatever our personal opinions on the relationship between the Christian faith and Marxism, it seems impossible to deny that the Marxist ideology and generally the related leftist groups have been the first to produce a consciousness of the need for social change in Latin America, and they have always been found in the vanguard of revolutionary changes. Latin American Marxism has not remained immune to the ideological conflict between Soviets and Chinese, between peaceful coexistence and the "permanent revolution." This controversy has become evident at least in the opposite positions of two Marxist groups. The promotion of "popular fronts," that is, the union of several more or less progressive parties within each country with electoral victory as the prime goal, is generally the policy of Moscow-oriented Communist Parties. The second position entails a much more belligerent attitude toward present structures and upholds the revolutionary strategy of a popular uprising through guerrilla warfare and the formation of a political consciousness among the peasants and working class. The controversy not only has divided Marxist groups in the hemisphere but has enfeebled the action of the entire left.

The only existing socialist experiment in Latin America also appears embroiled in this conflict as a result of its inevitable economic ties to the Soviet Union. Many observers of the Cuban Revolution interpret recent events as a sign that Cuba will be careful not to export the revolution to other countries in Latin America and, at the same time, will work toward a certain state of peaceful coexistence with the United States.

After the Cuban experience, guerrilla tactics seemed to revive considerable optimism among leftists as a possible road to power. We know that there are guerrillas in Guatemala, Venezuela, Colombia, Peru, and Bolivia and that in other countries small guerrilla revolts have appeared sporadically without further development. Information on these guerrilla groups is never adequate, but it seems clear that their possibilities of success, if they exist at all, are much less than those in the Cuban case. Latin American armies are at present especially equipped and trained to confront guerrillas, and the persecution they have unleashed is unrelenting. News dispatches try to create a special image of these guerrilla groups, with the result that the urban sector ends up identifying the guerrillas with mere bands of marauders. The controversy among leftists, previously discussed, has robbed them of the unanimous support of this latter group. In general, only university students and peasants in the areas where guerrillas are operating support them, while the urban populace remains largely indifferent to events. Needless to say, the foregoing analysis is admittedly sketchy and incomplete. Nevertheless, one cannot lose sight of the constant emergence of new leftist movements, even if they are hard to classify, which arise from the joint action of various ideological groups. Often, Christians and Marxists are found in these movements, displaying identical degrees of militancy.

The appearance of a new leftist nationalism in Latin American political thought has given rise, likewise, to the convergence of ideological positions regarded until recently as mutual opposites. The role of this nationalist ideology among the armed forces may be basic for the formulation of new revolutionary schemes.

We conclude here this account of the facts which have seemed to us most important for an understanding of what is happening today politically in the hemisphere. There still remains the exacting task of interpreting them more carefully; others may ascribe different meanings to these events.

There also remains—and this is most important—the responsibility not to subject oneself to the present scheme, but to study the roads that we may begin to follow tomorrow. This presentation ends, therefore, on a tentative note in order to allow this conference to realize the two indicated tasks and, as a fundamental concern, to seek to discover what the word of God may say to us in these circumstances.

We have tried to be realistic and to show that the prospects of immediate social change such as we all desire are dim. These changes will undoubtedly occur because they are the cause and the objective of an unrestrainable social pressure. An intelligent reading of history confirms this fact. But the birth pangs of the social revolution are greater than we formerly imagined. In spite of this, we must not forget that history moves at a stunning pace. The scheme we have just viewed may have become outdated in a few months by the advent of new facts capable of overturning this picture and of creating new conditions for social change. The paths of a revolutionary process are always novel and surprising.

It is highly possible that this conference will undertake its tasks in a much less self-assured mood than the preceding conferences, during which we insisted that social revolution was imminent. If our commitment to serve our neighbor in Latin America is genuine and if we come to understand that that service, in the context of today's Latin American poverty and misery, entails struggling for the transformation of the social environment, we can only examine reality as it is; and the fact is that that reality doesn't allow us to be optimistic.

---

1. Marcos Kaplan, "La Integración Latinoamericana y las Grandes Potencias," *Fichas de Investigación Económica y Social* (March, 1965).

2. Alberto Lleras Camargo, "Hay que salvar la Alianza," Progreso 65-66, special edition of *Visión* (1966), pp. 30-32.

3. "Los gorilas y las fronteras ideológicas," *Marcha* (Aug. 13, 1965).

3

A God Who Acts
and Renews His Church

Who but God is qualified to say what he is doing in his church, how and when he does it, and toward what end? A glance at the history of the church will suffice to check anyone's attempt to assume—or should we say usurp?—a prophetic role. When the First Vatican Council concluded its proceedings in the midst of a terrible storm, some declared, "You see, hell rages in vain impotence and indignation before the triumph of God"; and the others, "You see, the wrath of God cannot abide the atrocity of this heinous assembly." How contradictory are our interpretations! Was not John XXIII wiser in his interpretation of history when shortly before the Second Vatican Council he said to a close fellow churchman, "Well, what do you expect—when the Holy Spirit does something great in the Church, for the devil to go on vacation?" Isn't it much nearer the truth to say that the actions of God and the devil are so interwoven in history that only God himself can define his work?

God is his own interpreter. He has warned us against the temptation to act as impromptu philosophers of history: "It is not for you to know the times or seasons which the Father has fixed by his own authority" (Acts 1:7). What is God doing in Latin America today? Of what would a Jewish theologian have written around the year one A.D.? He would have referred to the Galilean revolt, the census of Tiberius, the decisions of the Sanhedrin, the development of rab-

---

This chapter is based on two lectures by José Míguez-Bonino.

binical schools, the Dead Sea sect, or, if he were very am-
bitious, the new religious and philosophical currents of the
Mediterranean world and the recent unification of the empire under Tiberius. Would it have occurred to him to mention a birth in Bethlehem or a carpenter of Nazareth whose
wife became pregnant before marriage?

Our subject is a challenge. This could very well be an
irresponsible venture, the possible source of great amuse-
ment to the serious professional historian as well as to the
Lord of history himself. The gift of prophecy is not subject
to our private custody nor to our conference agendas. Who-
ever presumes to exercise the gift without having first received it incurs the grave condemnation of false prophets:
"The prophets are prophesying lies in my name; I did not
send them, nor did I command them or speak to them. They
are prophesying to you a lying vision, worthless divination,
and the deceit of their own minds" (Jer. 14:14). ". . . they
are prophesying falsely in my name, with the result that I
will drive you out and you will perish, you and the prophets
who are prophesying to you" (Jer. 27:15). We would probably be wise to reflect upon the gravity of these words today
when we speak so freely of the "prophetic gift," of "discerning God's action," what God is doing here and there in the
church and in the world, East and West, as if we really
understood what a serious matter it is "to bear the word
of Yahweh."

Perhaps we should stop here, but that would be un-
justifiable: The unfathomability of God's action, his absolute sovereignty, and the mystery of his ways constitute
the first and last word of our task. God has not called an
advisory council, not even of clergymen, to help him govern
the world. But between this first and last word there are
certainly others—secondary, limited, ambiguous and precarious, but significant and necessary. These are simply the
words of the Christian theologian who does not presume

to have the gift of prophecy, but only the more modest call to find and refine theological concepts that help us to understand in biblical terms what is happening in the church and the world.

God has revealed to us the secret of his goal for human history, the mystery hidden from the beginning, as it is expressed in Ephesians 1—to unite all things under one head, Jesus Christ. The Scriptures witness to God's action in the history of his people in the world. The Bible, interpreted in the light of Jesus Christ, is the only standard for assessing contemporary events in terms of God's action and purpose. But let us not misunderstand each other. Jesus Christ is no magic formula, no secret clue which allows us to decipher the will of God or write a sacred philosophy of history. He is no general principle to be applied in interpreting particular cases. He is a decisive, concrete fact, one who does not "open" history to our understanding, but transforms, renews, and recreates it, placing us in it. For this reason it is so important for believers to "be" the history of God in the world before undertaking the ambiguous task of "interpreting" God's action. But that transforming action of God gives history its meaning and its goal. It is not that the history of Israel and Jesus Christ explains the meaning of history; rather, it creates it. Outside of Jesus Christ history has no meaning other than the "dust . . . to dust" idea of Genesis 3.

Nevertheless, the Bible may not be used for a direct analysis of our situation. We cannot draw exact parallels between its events and ours, given the sheer variety of biblical situations. And it is just as untenable to abstract general "principles" of interpretation, given the concrete nature of the Bible itself. Rather, biblical history may be related to our situation in the form of analogy or parables— as descriptions of God's action, which indirectly and by transposition are projected into our own history. The "indirectly" and "by transposition" point always to Christ. Therefore using the Bible in interpreting our circumstance demands a theological framework, a hermeneutic of the use of biblical analogies in understanding current circumstances. A theological task is a human deed, therefore fallible, risky, and highly debatable. But it is all we can and must do.

Hence, we shall devote the rest of the time to a presentation of useful theological tools for understanding what is happening in the church in Latin America today. In doing so, we wish to make allowance for three qualifications. First, theology concerns the proclamation of God's word *here* and *now;* therefore, we have taken as our starting point the current events in the churches of Latin America today— and let us not forget that that is the only reality: *churches.* The selection and identification of priorities have been, in effect, subjective (hopefully not arbitrary) and therefore debatable. Second, we have chosen only three of those theological instruments according to the situations in the church today which we considered most significant; the method may undoubtedly be expanded. Third, we have largely confined ourselves to Protestant churches, not because they are more important or more significant, but because they have given us this assignment and because they permit us to focus with greater concentration on elements which are also found in the Roman Catholic Church in other forms.

First Framework: The Growth and Strengthening of Christian Churches in Latin America

The fact of contemporary secularization of which we speak so often in "Church and Society," the alleged "de-Christianization" and "end of Christendom," neither contradict nor deny the growth and strengthening of Christian churches in Latin America. They are actually concomitants. Concurrent with the secularizing process, the churches in this hemisphere, as conscious functioning organisms, are growing in size and strength.

Protestant expansion has been sufficiently discussed and documented by Protestant, Catholic, and secular observers. The conditions and manner of growth vary greatly in different times and places. The most salient fact is the numerical growth: From 1937 to 1961 the number of Protestants in Latin America rose from 632,000 to 8,000,000, or from .5 to 5 percent of the total population, outstripping the world's highest rate of population increase.

This growth has also meant consolidation. In 1949 there were 10,971 ministers, 40 percent of them foreign; in 1961 of 41,089 ministers 15 percent were foreign.

The increase is also to be seen in the growing influence of Protestant professors and politicians whose number has reached considerable proportions in countries of a longer Protestant tradition.

Various factors are responsible for this Protestant expansion. Among the displaced rural proletariat moving into the cities of Chile and Brazil, the phenomenon is analogous to a skin rash spread by contagion; in Eastern Bolivia the method is service and presence amid people in agricultural colonization projects; in Central America the strategy is an unremitting battery of revivals.

But there has also been growth among Roman Catholics, which has not received equivalent documentation. The great myth of the homogeneous society of Catholic believers militates against such documentation. Realistically, though, considering the commitment of the community, the training and dedication of the clergy, the missionary activity of service, evangelization, teaching, and theological output, there has been an amazing growth from 1930 to the present.

Finally, in the last ten years there undeniably has been an increased concern with the church—new forms of receptivity and openness—on the part of the press, intellectual currents, etc. The nature of this interest is complex and ambiguous but quite real; it constitutes another indication of the growth of the church.

What analogical criteria does the Bible offer for evaluating this growth? We take as our prime example the classic on this matter: the Acts of the Apostles, an account which offers statistics on conversions and additions to the church (Acts 4:4; 5:14; 6:7; 11:21; 16:5).

According to this biblical picture, expansion is the work of God, his way of confirming the apostolic preaching, of authenticating their testimony and signs. Frequent reference is made to preaching with power, with the Spirit: The Lord "adds," the Spirit "convinces" or "converts," etc. Numbers are, in this context, evidence of the Lord's grace, of his favor toward men.

One must make use of predestinarian language to express the New Testament thought in this regard; the growth of the church reveals the antecedent purpose and hidden working of God in men: "I have a people," "I had many people," "those who were to be saved." Growth is a sign of the presence and activity of God. The modern heresy that the believers must be a minority is unheard of in the New Testament. Strictly speaking, this heresy is the result of inferring numerical minority from the insignificance of God's people. This perverts the gospel in the matter of central importance: salvation for all—that every man grow to the fullness of Christ (Col. 1:28)—which certainly means attaining faith and the community of faith.

Even the increase resulting from preaching of dubious motive is the gift of God (Phil. 1:15-18); even what comes from preachers of a different sort should be graciously received. (This is certainly the meaning of the passage concerning the disciples in Mark 9:38-41; at this point many of our objections to evangelistic and proselyting methods of doubtful purity will surely be raised.)

Expansion is, nevertheless, a confused issue, and its ambiguity is clearly seen in the growth of our churches, for which we give thanks to God and recognize his work. It is conspicuous how easily human curiosity and vanity forget the ultimately mysterious nature of that growth. This secret character is especially apparent in the preaching of Jesus: When growth is visible, his judgment on it is surprising; again, the parables of the Kingdom describe an imperceptible growth such that judgment remains a secret until the consummation.

The strange mixture of Protestant and sectarian expansion, the claim of exclusivism, and aggressive impulses toward a hostile society are further evidence of ambivalence. In this case we refer to the biblical example of Jesus' struggle with Phariseeism: "Woe to you, scribes and Pharisees, hypocrites! for you traverse sea and land to make a single proselyte, and when he becomes a proselyte, you make him twice as much a child of hell as yourselves" (Matt. 23:15). A good number of our forms of growth fall under that condemnation!

Finally, there is the danger of confusing growth with aggrandizement, of praising the mercy of God and being self-complacent with human grandeur. This is Isarel's fundamental problem (the census of Davis, the reign of Jeroboam II)—further proof of the ambiguous nature of growth.

Second Framework: Formation of a Growing Minority of People Transformed in Their Goals, Patterns of Behavior, and Criteria for Action in Latin America

The growth which we have been discussing is not simply a quantitative change, but the beginning of a new life made manifest in behavior and action. Even though the analysis is here confined to the Protestant Church, the same may be said of Roman Catholicism.

That the Scriptures consider this conversion the work of God needs no proof. Faith is born of repentance and expressed in obedience by walking in the ways of God, which always conflict with the ways of others. In the New Testament this discrepancy takes form in the confrontation between the Christian community and the pagan world. The new birth is manifest in a new life which is the work of the Spirit. The fruits which will be fully revealed on the last day (Phil. 1:10 f.) are now visible in three fundamental dimensions of life: the realm of life with others (love, generosity, kindness, and avoidance of anger, malice, profanity, etc.), the plane of personal freedom and spontaneity (joy, peace, trust), and the order of discipline for service (purity, truth, self-restraint, etc.). This new way of life does not consist of doled-out piecemeal virtues but constitutes the new life in Christ.

The new life is distinguished by its disparity with the form of this world—bondage, despair, anxiety, egotism, and wantonness, which are not miscellaneous vices, but an organic unity, the "old man," "the world," the former age and its fruits. The opposition of these two antithetical realities is an irreconcilable antagonism provoking hatred on the part of the world.

The apologetic role of this new life becomes especially evident near the end of the New Testament period (Phil. 2:14 f., 1 Peter 2, etc.), as this new life reveals the nature and reality of the gospel. The biblical picture before us can help us understand a very important aspect of the life of the church in Latin America. The effects of the gospel in the sobriety, the honesty, and the diligence of the evangelist and in the esteem with which he is regarded have lent themselves to his prompt social advancement. There are still more profound results: the end to alienation in the community of believers, the releasing of joy, spontaneity, singing, and personal creativity. Furthermore, the apologetic value of this new life and its positive contribution to the life of our people cannot be ignored. Once again, however, there appear in spite of these benefits the works of the flesh, which Scripture regards as the Satanic caricature of the new life and which the history of Latin American churches abundantly illustrates.

In the early church Paul, who by the Spirit was able to describe so richly the life in Christ, fought doggedly against the diabolical deformation of that life by Judaizing forces which would reduce it to faith in works, as valuable in and of themselves, and as the works of man rather than the gift and manifestation of the Spirit. The signs of a radical Judaizing of the life in Christ are patent in our Latin American churches. In Pauline terms these are the signs: boasting (*kauchema*), confidence in the virtues of Protestantism and conviction of its superiority, the popularity of books in this vein such as Hoffet's *Protestant Imperialism;* second, legalism—the ethics of "dos" and "don'ts" according to which a person is judged—which amounts to the dehumanization of the new life; finally, intolerance by Latin American Protestant sectarianism of those whom Paul calls "weak."

This Judaizing adulteration is aggravated in Latin America by a force which Paul faced in his own time: The very norms proffered for adoption arise from a particular national heritage (Jewish) whose divine origin Paul did not dispute, but which in light of the gospel had been cast aside to make way for new forms (Paul's use of catalogues of pagan virtues). We have done a cruder job of Judaizing by making typical Protestant norms—or even worse, simply Anglo-Saxon customs—the standards for manifestation of the new life; the results are artificiality, disorientation, and a confusion of Christ and culture.

If the foregoing be true, then the outward appearances and traditions of current Christianity which we are often tempted to write off as outmoded and decadent reveal, nevertheless, signs of the presence of the Holy Spirit, the action of the Triune God, the power of the resurrected and triumphant Christ. But we have also seen that these same deeds exhibit the traits which Scripture attributes to Satan, to the flesh, and to natural man—symptoms of human arrogance, conceit, and self-centeredness.

One might paradoxically say that the life of the churches reveals the presence of the triumphant Christ who calls and sustains his own while that presence is constantly being denied by the tendency of our churches to forget the identity of the Crucified and Risen One: the signs of the Cross in the midst of the victory. For orthodox traditional Christianity in Latin America, the call to discern and to be shaped by God's work should be a call to receive and reveal the power and victory of Jesus Christ in the self-denial of the Suffering Servant.

The churches are growing; a community of believers is being formed. These facts describe what is taking place in the church as empirical phenomena, intrinsic to its presence. We have found that these facts are ambiguous and that in biblical terms we can rightly see through them not only the work of the Holy Spirit but also the subversion of Satan. At the same time, there is an equally important extrinsic phenomenon which conditions the forms expressive of the being and presence of the churches. This we shall examine briefly as "The Openness of Christian Churches in Latin America." The term "openness" is clearly being used in a metaphorical sense in the same way that we speak of a person or group being open or of an open dialogue, that is, readiness to expand one's horizons and receptivity in the realms both of action and of ideas and attitudes.

Among the various forces which bring about openness in the churches, we should mention first, because of chronology not priority, international influences, especially those from beyond the hemisphere. The complex phenomenon which we habitually misname the "ecumenical movement" comes immediately to mind: the International Missionary Council, the World Council of Churches, the World Christian Student Federation, the Young Men's Christian Association, and other organizations which have helped promote this opening. Apart from the traditional tendency of our countries to take their lead from Europe, new channels to freedom from the almost exclusive and overpowering influence of the United States are opened through literature, travel, scholarships and exchanges, European theological ideas, concern for Asian unity, post-war restoration movements.

Denominational ties which extend beyond Latin America constitute another factor. The Presbyterian churches afford a good contemporary example. Something similar may be said of the 1961 Conference at El Tabo, Chile, and the study guide on the mission of the church which was debated and accepted; the 1965 Lutheran Conference in Lima (Professor Trillhaas' lectures); and denominational literature committed to the worldwide ecumenical theological movement.

One might suppose that this affects only the so-called liberal denominations (a term as inadequate as it is imprecise). Viewed more realistically, however, one would have to include the Association of Evangelicals, Evangelical Literature for Latin America, and Billy Graham's crusades, even if they fall into a different category. It is true that the latter bear the negative connotations of exclusivism toward other Protestant groups and reaction to what they consider a distortion of or threat to sound doctrine. But we should not belittle the type of bonds which they create nor the new openings in the field of fundamentalist theology, including such names as Roman, Carnell, etc. The Baptists are producing renewal missions; following the lead of missionaries, the seminaries are now open to new theological ideas. We could cite names and places, but that is unnecessary for our purposes.

We should include one additional element: the influences from outside the hemisphere which have been opening new and unimagined horizons for Roman Catholicism in Latin America. The Second Vatican Council dramatized the new forces already at work. Latin American students have been trained in Italy, Germany, Belgium, and France. Dominican and Jesuit priests stand out in initiating reforms here. New developments in Catholic theology are occurring under Schmaus, Rahner, von Balthasar, Congar, etc.

Another impulse toward new openings has arisen from the present social conditions of our actual environment. Church events, considered in this context, encompass the changes throughout the whole of society, an analysis which we will not undertake in order to avoid duplication. It may be said, nevertheless, that the awakening to rapid social change and to new social conditions in Latin America is the most salient feature of our historical juncture. Certain data have become common knowledge: The percentage of the population which is going hungry, the rate of population growth, the distribution of wealth, and the revolutionary climate are recurrent topics. The way in which this atmosphere has penetrated even the most unreceptive groups and stirred up interest is remarkable.

The great cultural levelers, mass communications—radio, television, motion pictures, the press—have contributed to the diffusion of these facts, opening before man a local and worldwide panorama of reality in which he is involved.

Urbanization has the same effect of integrating him into the whole of life.

Another factor is the internationalization of life through the ideological claims of the international power blocs, which cannot be ignored. The United Nations and propaganda networks force us to take cognizance of remote events which we would otherwise ignore: Vietnam, India, Pakistan, Rhodesia. This not only affects the educated elite but extends even to the reader of the comic strips.

The inner dynamics of the churches are integrally involved in this process of opening, making possible the assimilation of these facts and serving as the solvent of this set of factors. We have reached the second and third generations of Protestants, who are rooted in national life with a great sense of belonging, of responsibility, and of nationality.

The cultural and social situation of that second or third generation Protestant has opened new horizons for him and, at the same time, has awakened the desire (very human and sinful) to "belong" to this world and spurred a new interest in that reality; it thus becomes possible for him to assimilate the movements we have discussed.

In Catholicism the process of de-Christianization has created an inner stalemate which has raised a real concern over the loss of the masses. In Protestantism the lack of success or the slowing of the pace in some places has had the same effect of producing a new source of concern. Even the Pentecostals have developed such an attitude in response to the loss of the second generation.

This openness which we have just described has produced several movements which we usually term "renewal" but which, at any rate, express the desire for modification or transformation. It is sufficient simply to mention them without going into a detailed description.

In the first place, Latin American Christianity, Protestantism in particular, has suffered a sharp division and a splintering tendency. In addition to traditional divisions originating in the home nations of the missionary churches (primarily the United States and England) and in their own native dissension, other elements compound the difficulties: the separatism and isolationism characteristic of the majority of churches which came to Latin America, the tensions between conservatives and revolutionaries in a changing society, interregional frictions within the hemisphere (the Río de la Plata, the Pacific, etc.), conflicts between foreigners and nationals aggravated by such issues as nationalism and imperialism, and important theological differences (real or imagined)—for example, between fundamentalism and modernism. The factors for openness mentioned once before have acted as unifying forces for the Congress of Panama to the Latin American Conferences: Latin American Union of Protestant Youth, the conciliar movements, the work of the Student Christian Movement, the dialogue between Protestants and Roman Catholics, etc. All of these, however, proceed from the same base, from international influences and the trend toward ecumenical unity.

Various factors have converged to consolidate and intensify the quest for unity: the new sense of nationality, the challenge of concrete tasks (evangelization, service, literary production, theological education), and the stimulus of Roman Catholic renewal. The question has led to a real struggle between ecumenists and anti-ecumenists but not over isolation, since one concept of unity is always combated in the name of another. Thus the World Council of Churches is countered by "fundamentalism," and the national unions by the united confessional families. The attraction of unity is a force inherent in the dynamics of churches; the point is to determine the direction, the patterns, the means, and the scope of the unity to be achieved.

There is a second factor which is difficult to consider objectively but which must be included because of its decisive importance: the struggle for indigenization of the churches (including the Roman Catholic). Latin American Protestantism has suffered from the practice of planning, executing, and evaluating its affairs in terms of a general scheme conceived abroad rather than in the setting of local realities. The local scene has been considered not as a significant reality, but as an aggregate of individuals uprooted from their environment and joined to a new entity—the church—regarded as "extraterritorial" in relation to its field of operations and "territorial" in relation to its homeland. The dominant role of the foreigner led necessarily to this type of situation.

The concern for nationalism, which plays a vital part in Latin American thinking, is creating a new outlook. With it have come serious tensions, particularly with the emergence of national leadership in the churches. These tensions tend to take different forms in the spheres of training, governing "status," and economics; but they reach at times a state of extreme hostility, complicated especially by the general Latin American scene of marked anti-Yankee reactions among certain sectors (above all the University) in which Protestantism is beginning to take root. These tensions and conflicts should not, however, conceal from us the real nature of the movement, corresponding essentially to the awakening of a national consciousness and sense of personal responsibility, to the "appropriation" of the church and its ingrafting into the actual local matrix.

In this section it is unnecessary to develop the theme of social concern, since that is the business of the whole aggregate of presentations made here. It is interesting to observe the reception of the work of the nascent commissions of Church and Society in different parts of the continent and of the central organization which sustains them. This reception has enabled them to attain in five years a degree of influence which other cooperative efforts have not gained in half a century. The Latin American Protestant—be he Methodist or Pentecostal, Bolivian or Uruguayan—feels that the realities confronting his faith pertain to his whole being and determine his mission. The movement still lacks theological maturation and local anchoring, but we have before us the matrix of true ecumenical encounter, at once substantial and fruitful.

Finally we mention the concern over church structures— recently among Roman Catholics also—produced by the impact of openness. The concern is primarily with the "inadequacy" of present structures, owing to their foreign origin, age, and irrelevance. A second element of this concern is for the congregational structure which, although imported also, becomes so crucial to our environment due to the urbanization process that our churches reflect the self-enclosed type of parish. What structure accords with the missionary nature of the church? What framework promotes openness to the world for the sake of service? What form corresponds to the realities of our society? What type of pattern reflects the "servant" nature of Jesus Christ and his identification with the needy and the searching?

The forms of ministry (lay, professional, specialized) and denominational and interdenominational organization are likewise sources of concern. We should already have mentioned the recent innovations in theology and teaching, that is, a biblical and educational reformation which expresses the search for new ways to awaken Christian people to the total meaning of their faith in all its dimensions.

We have seen the factors of openness which provide

opportunities for renewal of biblical and theological thinking in the churches, new modes of relationship and influence with each other, a vital interchange with the environment, structural renovation and new life patterns. How
are we to understand and assess all this from a biblical
standpoint? We here wish to propose for our special consideration two points of special relevance to the specific
concerns of Church and Society.

The first problem is the "institutionalization" of the
churches, taken in this case to mean something different
from the usual rendering. The Latin American churches
are not "missions" (expansion movements based elsewhere),
nor are they conformed to being mere "parts." Rather, they
seek to establish themselves, find a structure of their own,
set up their own base of operations, open themselves to vital
personal relationships with their environment, and establish
their own centers for thought and study. We are calling
this search for maturity "institutionalization" in the sense of
"instituting or establishing oneself."

The second point is closely related to the first; it is the
question of the relationship between the church and the
world around it. In a sense it is the problem underlying
the whole Church and Society movement, for which reason
the actual not simply theoretical, theological basis of this
issue is decisive. Here the conflict between the pietist-funda-
mentalist tradition and the liberalizing forces leads to an
understanding of the theological relation between church
and "world"—which includes the concepts of salvation,
Christian life, even ecclesiology. This is the vital theological
link.

What biblical analogies can help us understand these
problems? Let us suggest two which are in a certain sense
parallel and therefore the most appropriate. The first analogue is the *establishment of the monarchy in Israel* at the

beginning of the ninth century B.C. Someone has said half jokingly that the best description of Protestantism in Latin America is given about Israel in the book of Judges: "In those days there was no king in Israel; every man did what was right in his own eyes" (Judg. 17:6).

The basic problem of the institution of the monarchy is the inadequacy of Israel in her new environment, on changing from a nomadic to an agricultural way of life and encountering more advanced institutions. If Israel is to function well (in terms of an age of wars and alliances), she must acquire an appropriate structure (indigenous and effectual), which entails internal organization and adjustments. But with Israel, the people of God, structural change is not a simple matter of environment and expedience: How does this affect her relationship with God? Structure is not neutral when it pertains to God's people. How can this new relation be understood in terms of the "covenant"?

One must here recall the dual interpretation which makes the new situation ambiguous: God grants the monarchy to meet Israel's need: "He shall save my people ... because their cry has come to me" (1 Sam. 9:15-17). It is an instrument of God's rule, of his mercy and divine providence, but also a sign of rebelliousness, of the quest for human security, "like the nations"; insofar as it replaces Yahweh himself, it is an act of disobedience (1 Sam. 8).

In its actual functioning also the monarchy turned out to be ambivalent. It revealed the ultimate plan of God, prefigured in the kingship of David, and embodied the great risk—baalization, accepting just "like other nations" the criteria set by institutional monarchy: the Baalist values and concept of the nation, even to the point of calling Yahweh "Baal."

When this happens, how should we respond? As the Rechabites, "back to the desert," to nomadic life? The prophetic reply, on the other hand, is based on the *covenant* and *eschatology*: The earthly king cannot be supreme; God rules, and his reign is his deed.

The second analogue is *the rupture between nascent Christianity and Judaism* during the apostleship of Paul. The Greco-Roman world regarded Christianity as simply a Jewish sect, one among many. Is not this the situation of Protestantism in Latin America? Are we sects of Anglo-Saxon Protestantism or the Church of Jesus Christ in Latin America, legitimately and authentically established by God in this place?

Paul does not disavow the Jewish roots; he even reminds the Gentiles that from them stem the covenant, the law, the promises . . . But Christians are not a sect; they are the people of God. Being a Jew is not a prerequisite for belonging to Christ. The uniqueness of the Christian church lies not in Judaism, but in Jesus Christ. It creates its own religious forms in every place and in every age, none of which saves but Christ in them (and even in spite of them). Undoubtedly there arose in that time of acute Hellenization and diffusion of Gnostic creeds the same ambivalence found in our present situation.

Of course we cannot begin to apply these analogues literally; for that reason they are guides, not models to be imitated. Openness is an incision which God makes in our lives to free us from bondage and revitalize the mission entrusted to the church in this time and place. We must recognize the providential nature of that incision as Paul does in setting the Gentiles free from the covenant obligations imposed by Jewish tradition. Only such reforms can reveal the nature of the gospel. Our situation, while obviously different, is an extension of the same development, the unfolding of God's grace and creativity in the "full number of the Gentiles" (Rom. 11:25).

What are the "Judaic laws"? The churches must discover them from their existential situations: denominations, inherited liturgies, theological schools, institutional structures, forms of ministry. But the Pauline paradox must not be forgotten: The Jewish heritage is the history of God and his people, which cannot be discounted. That past can neither prohibit access to Christ nor insure union with him. God has freed the churches from such bondage to the past.

This liberation is in terms of openness to an existential situation, to our Latin American reality with all its features, its needs, its institution, and its personality or personalities. The liberation affects at least three realms of church life: the problem of theological renewal of thought patterns consonant with changing circumstances, the need to establish priorities or at least take into consideration the order of claims made upon us by social demands as distinguished from church concerns, the question of the nature and forms of our relationship to the world which will authenticate the task of evangelization.

But let us not forget that Satan takes no vacation; the paradox which makes for his presence is found also among us. The problem of the "baalization" of Israel is at work today in the confrontation of church and "world."

We must remember that the church is not the correlate of society's anxieties and hopes, confessed or hidden; it neither takes its criteria from nor renders an account to society. In this respect we need a theology of church and world faithful to the complete biblical witness. We gravitate between two heresies: the fundamentalist heresy, which tends to ignore the fact that Christ reconciled the world to himself, and the currently emergent heresy which disregards the call to faith, conversion, decision, and biblical eschatology. The latter seems to ignore the existence of sin and the necessary difference which faith makes in life;

it speaks carelessly, "impressionistically," of identification and incarnation without seeking the true meaning of these biblical affirmations. Reading Philippians 2 may help us grasp the dangers involved here. The gospel is always conscious of the need for differentiation from and rejection of the world. The community dispersed in the world does not exist without the community congregated and set apart, without which there is nothing to disperse but "salt without flavor" and barren yeast.

Therefore, the signs of change should be viewed critically: Not all revolutionary fervor is the work of God; not all the emphasis on the laity and de-emphasis on the clergy results in the priesthood of believers; not all ecumenism means unity of the body of Christ; not all theological concern is obedience to the Word of God; not all indigenization is God's sowing in our soil.

Denis de Rougemont once said that the devil is the absolute antitype, in that his nature is precisely disguise, the usurpation of appearances, the blatant or subtle bluff —in a word, the art of making forms lie. The devil never creates but only corrupts. All history, including our own, occurs therefore in the realm of ambiguity; at every moment we run the risk of trying to isolate the devil in one current and God in the other. Where God creates, he opens the door to the devil: "Watch and pray that you may not enter into temptation" (Matt. 26:41).

4

... And a God Who Acts
and Transforms History

Any attempt to think theologically on social and political realities today is found to be riddled with difficulties. A biblical scholar may accuse us of slighting exegesis, while some systematic theologians think this apologetic endeavor for clarity sounds more like sociology than theology. Not even the sociologist is impressed, since he proceeds from the precept of the primacy of empirical investigation. Even within the Christian community there arise almost insurmountable difficulties. In the first place, the majority of believers of the older generation find it impossible to understand why we wish to discard the traditional categories and expressions of faith in favor of new ones; on the other hand, many members of the younger generations, influenced greatly by the process of secularization, have reached the conclusion that theology lacks all meaning. In the face of this situation, perhaps we would do best to reexamine the meaning of theology for us today. Why is this problem so critical? There are several reasons which we should consider.

Almost all the traditional theological terms, including those which refer to God, salvation, etc., are now identified with an outdated view of the world and no longer bear any meaning for those occupied with present realities. They belong, in general, to a metaphysical age in which the central

---

This chapter is based on two lectures by Richard Shaull.

affirmations of the Christian faith pertained to a transcendental Eternal Order outside the temporal realm. In this day and age, men are directing their attention more and more to their concrete, historical existence. That dualistic outlook on life has disappeared, and with it, all possibility of expressing Christianity in such terms. From another standpoint the majority of our modes of expressing the gospel belong to the religious sphere, which was for ages at the center of human existence. Nevertheless, all that has changed today. As Bonhoeffer foresaw, religion in our day has become for many people a compartmentalized experience, completely marginal to daily life. Moreover, as long as we continue to talk of God and the transcendent in metaphysical terms, we contribute to a situation in which many of those with strong church ties are forced to believe that Christian faith has lost all meaning.

In Church and Society in Latin America our theological discussions have centered largely around *God's action in history*. This has made it possible for us to depart from certain stagnant theological concepts, examine our historical situation theologically, and thus make significant progress in correlating our Christian heritage and the world in which we live. Even here, unfortunately, we have faced serious difficulties. Insofar as our concept of God remains bound to a metaphysical concept of the world, our discussion of the meaning of his action in history becomes unintelligible. Those of us with neoorthodox theological background tend to speak of God's action in primarily theological and philosophical terms, which appear too abstract for those who wish to interpret this meaning in the midst of a revolutionary process. First we demand that they learn our vocabulary and think in our terms and then adapt their apprehension of reality to our scheme. Some people have tried to do this in the past; it is doubtful whether the future is with them.

The most distinctive feature of the secular interpretation of the world is its radically historical nature. Modern man tends to focus on his existence within this temporal and spatial framework as a member of the social order. He may be anxious over *ultimate* questions, but these are not what we would usually call "religious." Rather, they focus on the future—on the possibilities for transforming society and finding personal meaning and fulfillment through participation in that struggle. Consequently, these questions are definitely theological. But theological reflection on historical reality cannot be carried out independently and abstractly by the theologian. On the contrary, it should involve the aspects of reality under consideration with the appropriate specialized tools of the social and psychological sciences. Thus, theological reflection implies two tasks: interpretation of biblical and theological tradition as such and reflection on its contemporary meaning, a facet to be carried out in dialogue with specialists in the empirical sciences.

Although the task of theology may be difficult, it is not impossible; besides, it is of prime importance owing to the limitations of the social sciences. Empirical analysis works best when the historical process is broken in upon and a particular moment or limited period of time comes under consideration. However, it cannot answer man's questions about the future. The sociologist can examine what happens to man, but he cannot determine what is or what accounts for the human quality of life. Sociology studies the effects of values in human life, but it cannot decide what those values should be. If modern man feels the need to orient himself confidently and responsibly toward the future, he must find some framework which gives meaning and value to historical reality. Only then can study enlighten his spirit and strengthen his will for the struggle to transform the world. Such an orientation was made possible in the past by the great all-encompassing systems of thought which aimed at a synthesis of all man's knowledge and experience. Today we no longer have such confidence in the powers of reason. Nor do we believe that the dynamic reality of history can be incorporated into such a system in any useful way. Today truth is sought by means of certain clues for interpreting reality, within well defined spheres, which will prove adequate guides for our thought and action. But the clues are constantly changing, so that the quest for truth becomes a perpetual movement of partial success, failure, and renewal. This quest forces us to work out ideologies that define our future goals and the means by which we hope to achieve them, but in such a way that revision and reworking become constant.

In these terms the problem may turn out much to the liking of the theologian, because the Christian heritage does not give us today an all-inclusive system, but a specific perspective on human life and history through which man may find self-realization and meaning in life. It is a way of understanding *our history* in the light of the specific history of Israel and of Jesus Christ. It is a description of humanity and of the possibilities of humanization revealed in Jesus of Nazareth, as experienced in relationship with him and as interpreted by biblical images and parables.

We need not prove the superiority of this perspective nor insist on its authority. It is simply the legacy which we have received and which we may regard as one option within our experience. In such a manner this legacy establishes its legitimacy, and it is validated in our daily struggle to act responsibly in each situation we meet. For by the biblical interpretation of revelation we possess no esoteric truth to impose upon life, but something of an intimation imparted to us for understanding what is happening in history. Revelation means the unveiling of hidden reality. Our task, therefore, is not to impose certain values, but to discover and live by those governing the world; it is not to give but to discover the meaning of life in a world which shares in redemption; it is not to order the universe, but to participate in the new order taking shape through social transformation.

Any attempt to relate this heritage to our contemporary situation will be difficult, not only because the world has changed considerably since that time, but also because biblical history, like our own, is so varied and rich that the selection of clues for interpreting and appropriating the meaning of events, of that day and our own, turns out to be very complicated. Nevertheless, the possibility of interpretation depends upon the formulation of precisely that hermeneutic criterion. This is a risky business. No principle will be completely adequate, and even the most apt principles will be useful only as long as they are constantly renewed. There is, however, no alternative to carrying out this task; otherwise we would be limited to selecting from the Bible the parables, concepts, and analogies which seem most suitable to us and our situation. This arbitrary approach to biblical history would only plunge us into greater confusion.

Is it possible to find a criterion of interpretation which would enable us to relate the entire biblical message to our present human situation? Professor Paul Lehman has suggested the following possibility: *The biblical message describes the way in which God acts to grant and sustain the "human" condition of man.* More specifically, the Bible is the herald of the open opportunities for man to attain his full maturity and to fulfill his capacity for relationship by participating in the work of transforming the world. In these terms, there are two facts which distinguish the Christian position. One is the affirmation that man has the possibility of realizing his humanity, because his life forms part of a sovereign or autonomous situation. Life is basically response, acceptance of the gift of what man could not attain on his own. This revolutionary concept of life within the process of history originated in the experience of the people of Israel. Again and again in its national life the people were challenged by a presence which was beyond their comprehension but to which they had to respond. The biblical concept of God as Yahweh—"I am who I am"—grew out of this position.

Our Christian concept of transcendence is also a result of this experience. We affirm that in the midst of our history moving forward into the future, we must constantly confront this sovereign force, this transcendence that meets us here, in this life, and now, in present history. And experience teaches us that in response to him who confronts us in the midst of history, we discover our complete freedom to actualize our existence in the world.

The second central Christian affirmation is that this ultimate reality which transcends us is revealed to us by *grace*. Biblical faith offers no rational reply to the problem of suffering and evil but limits itself to testimonies of the unexpected manifestations of grace which are granted us here in this life. It shows us how the powers that enslave men individually and collectively are destroyed and man is set free to fulfill the possibilities of his life.

We repeat that all this is only an attempt to discover the expression in contemporary terms of the central fact of the biblical message. In his studies of the forms of God's action in the Bible, Professor Beato of Brazil has referred to the Old Testament as Israel's reflection on the pivotal events of her history: the exodus, the promised land, etc. And he has shown us that the people of Israel were gripped by the encounter with an active presence in their midst which they could not evade. The covenant supremely expressed this idea of life as response, as a calling which sets the course and destiny of the nation. Furthermore, this popular sovereignty sprang from the initiative of grace; Israel left behind her slavery and the events of the exodus in pursuit of the promised land and freedom. Historical existence meant participation in a redemptive process in which she could expect new events at any moment.

As Professor Beato has shown, this fact bore enormous consequences. It led Israel to regard the realms of nature and history as equally part of God's creation and thus freed her from the predominant persuasion of the ancient world which led to sacralizing the world. It also freed Israel to reject the cyclical concept of history and to see history moving toward the consummation of an ultimate purpose for man.

The doctrine of the Trinity likewise represents, not a mysterious and incomprehensible notion, but an attempt to describe the nature of the presence which we encounter in life and history making available a structure adapted to human experience. This doctrine affirms that the created order lies ultimately in the hands of him who has expressed his redemptive purpose and whose activity continues through the medium of history to its final completion. The will visibly revealed in Jesus of Nazareth is the clue to understanding the ultimate goal and power that move the universe. The Spirit who redeems life and renews human experience is the same Spirit who moves history.

This same perspective is revealed in the traditional Christological formulations. Unfortunately, theological efforts to face this problem came more or less to a standstill following the endeavor of Chalcedon to describe correctly the relation between the two natures. Aside from all this, however, there was a latent element first pointed out by Leontius of Byzantium in his affirmation of the enhypostasia: The human nature of Jesus is *in* the divine nature. The human nature of Jesus was real precisely because he was *in God;* Jesus had his humanity in God. We assume this means that when we consider the fulfillment of humanity in the man Jesus of Nazareth, we must confess that Jesus Christ is truly man because in him our humanity, which does not exist apart autonomously, is fully realized. Christ reveals the possibility of reaching human fullness, a gift which we can receive when we move toward the future openly and expectantly.

What then do we conclude from all this? If we are not to construct a Christian system to be imposed on reality and if all the traditional categories for expressing the meaning of faith are no longer adequate, what do we have left? One possible conclusion is that our main problem is not the reality of God and his action, but our conceptualization of it. We lack the terms to describe or even indicate it, but still more seriously we are often so alienated in our religious life, so remote from the sphere of his action, that we have almost no opportunity to perceive or describe what he is *now.* Therefore, we must first learn how to be present in the contemporary struggle of man, in the frontiers where this struggle is being carried out, and there try to maintain a vital interchange between the Christian definition of humanity and history and our existential situation as we experience and understand it. Out of this approach there may arise new patterns of theologizing and new images, concepts, and parables more capable of describing in completely secular terms how God is at work in our midst.

To inform our theological thinking in the manner suggested, we must work with some very concrete human problems. A recent Church and Society publication, *Man, Ideology and Revolution in Latin America,* attempted this in considering the concept of development and its implicit historical nature. Rather than repeat those observations, we shall examine another problem: the meaning of the freedom, maturity, and fulfillment of man—concepts which will serve as the basis for further discussion.

Paul Lehman has coined a phrase to describe the central message of the gospel: *what God is doing in the world to make and to keep life human.* His description of what it means to be human seems quite acceptable, but we must emphasize an additional point: The context in which the humanization process takes place has changed greatly as a result of the transition from a relatively stable and static, otherworldly, metaphysical order to the dynamic, secular, future-oriented society of today. In the former case human life was transformed and given its meaning in accordance with its integration into the eternal order, a process in which it was disciplined and perfected. In the present situation the transformation and the meaning of life are found in a precarious passage to maturity and toward a total realization in the future. This can occur only when the bonds of all the old and new absolutes along with all forms of authoritarianism are cast aside and man is freed to develop in an attitude of trust and hope. Let us look at this contrast in more specific terms.

In the past, human life could be truly human as it was integrated with the all-embracing concept of Being based on the eternal order. Human existence had solid foundations; man had his *place*, stable and secure. In Bonhoeffer's words, man had solid ground under his feet. Our problem today is how to adjust the radically historical nature of our existence to constant change—how to be free to live without the old security, without depending on ultimate grounds in the traditional fashion.

In an earlier age, man attained a higher degree of humanity through religion, that is, recognizing the sacred nature of all the realms that ordered his life and respecting the existing authority structures in each of these orders. At present, we come to a fuller understanding of humanity only according to the measure of our secularization, of our freedom to see beyond the myths which man has created and through which he has lived, of our realization of the frailty of social institutions and the precariousness of man's existence. The person who can accept change and rejoice in the implicit new possibilities for honesty and openness is already on his way to a fuller human life.

Formerly, religion was a humanizing agent insofar as it disciplined life by controlling unrestrained passions and anarchic tendencies in man. This was possible due to the general recognition of certain ideals and moral norms and the church's means of effectively disciplining a man and urging him on to a higher life. At present there are no generally valid and accepted norms. Moreover, in the march toward the future within the concrete historical situation, man's chance to live is constantly threatened by all those limiting prohibitions. Reaching a fuller humanity means being free to break out of those bonds. Discipline is as necessary as ever today, but it is possible only when life is oriented and directed toward the form of future things.

In a metaphysical age human life acquired meaning through integrating all fields of knowledge into a generalizing synthesis from which the correct interpretation of every event in each particular order of experience was to have been deduced. Today we gain access to truth when we have the freedom to open ourselves to new things and the courage to unite the fragments of our knowledge in different spheres and disciplines, hoping for new but still precarious possibilities of meaning and interpretation.

In the past, man's social existence became more fully

human by means of the institutions which preserved past accomplishments and guaranteed the stability of present relations. Today social life can become human only through change in the institutional structures. Order is the relationship between men and institutions which is worked out and continuously refined after the actual change.

In summary, the humanizing process formerly was grounded in loyalty to God as center and upholder of a religious and metaphysical order. Presently, in Gabriel Vahanian's terms, that same process depends on the choice between iconoclasm and idolatry. In this context the challenge to Christianity is to pronounce the *liberating word* —to offer signs and symbols in word and flesh of the radical freedom which is now man's in a secular world, to move on to a new meaning and fulfillment of life. And, if we understand the gospel correctly, this is precisely what we should be ready to do, because the central affirmation of Christian tradition is that man's existence stands in the context of sovereignty and grace, in which freedom is seen as a gift which he can make his own and by which he can live.

In spite of the severe problems he faces, if man is at present really en route from slavery to the promised land and freedom, we all have a well-defined task to carry out. Our duty is to enter, on behalf of man's future, into the very heart of the struggle where the most critical issues of humanization or dehumanization are rooted and to seek there the symbols or images which can bear the liberating word. Simultaneously we must adopt a style of life which will make this freedom contagious. Because wherever word and action are combined in this type of vital engagement, individuals and communities are able to face each day concrete decisions which lead them to appropriate and live the freedom possible for all men. It is sufficient here to mention briefly a few dimensions of this fact.

Man has the freedom to live and learn from the past without being dominated by it. Our past is both a legacy and a burden to us. As a legacy, the past may be preserved as a contribution to the present, stripped of its absoluteness and transformed by incorporation into our experience. Since the power of the old authority structures has been destroyed, we need no longer subject ourselves to them nor define our identity in terms of opposition to them. We can accept the responsibility for our past—for example, by recognizing our guilt while simultaneously finding forgiveness and the strength to face that guilt and bear it. Most important, we may discover that our lives and thoughts are oriented toward specific future goals, becoming one in them.

The problem is that many people are not ready to accept this type of freedom. They are unable to face the unforeseeable possibilities in each decision or to find the resources for self-discipline when all the external controls are gone. They prefer, therefore, to transfer their responsibility to a group, an organization, or a law that does everything for them. If our analysis of events in the contemporary world was correct, any attempt to continue in this line becomes in the end dehumanizing and enslaving. The church particularly should resist the temptation to use religion or the religious community toward this end. On the contrary, the task awaiting us is to discover how the church can encourage those who have not reached this degree of maturity to acquire greater initiative, discipline, and responsibility.

In the Christian perspective human life is freed from the inhibiting power of circumstance. Man can understand the meaning of the circumstantial as an inherent element in historical existence where we are constantly being met by grace.

One of the strange ironies of our time is the fact of having freed ourselves from the supernatural forces that once dominated man's life, only to become the victims of circumstance. In the course of events it is easy to give circumstantial events unmerited importance, to let ourselves become obsessed with them and make them into major obstacles to fully realizing the significance of life.

In this case also, Christian faith has the opportunity to pronounce the liberating word. Everything that happens belongs to the created order. Circumstance must be stripped of its sacred and religious qualities and considered realistically. Furthermore, circumstance represents the realm in which grace works, the field in which the redemptive God acts to unify what is scattered, to restore life's order, and to open new possibilities where the old seem drained. In relation to circumstance, our freedom is the freedom to respond to grace; in other words, the attitude of confidently awaiting new opportunities when circumstances seem adverse and taking advantage of every experience—no matter how limited and fleeting—in which the meaning of events and the possibilities of full personal realization give us strength to face the future with hope.

We are free also to probe the depths of the contemporary crisis in our society and to discover in it new possibilities for social reconstruction and human reconciliation. One of the most disturbing signs in the present situation is the fact that the majority of our governments are identified with a status quo policy at a time in which the most profound schisms are appearing in the face of our continent. Quite often events shock us into realizing the degree of suffering and injustice we have tolerated in our society. No matter what the final outcome of the present struggle, the newly emergent forms of life are bound to shake up our bourgeoise mentality and perhaps horrify us. Probably the most difficult task is to face the situation honestly; we are too often tempted to smooth things over to fool ourselves, an attitude which naturally aggravates the situation.

Nevertheless, we have an alternative. Those attentive to

the crucifixion of the God-Man and the biblical description of human rebellion can face reality as it is without difficulty. In the light of Christ's victory over evil and his permanent ministry of uniting all things in himself, the worst cases of human degeneracy and exploitation of man by man become an occasion for human renewal and social transformation. And for those who recall the consequences of Christ's presence among publicans and sinners and the astonishment at God's actions, there is no reason to fear the new forms of life and liberty which may emerge in time.

5

Christian Community
and Contemporary Secularization

In the last few decades Christians have become increasingly and dramatically aware of secularization. This is one of the most important phenomena of our time, affecting in many ways the life and mission of the church. Without pretending to give the total picture of this process nor all the consequences of its impact on the Christian community, we will try to show the repercussions of this Christian awakening, paying particular attention to its effects on the organization and structure of the Christian community.

Our procedure will be as follows: first, a survey of the facts currently characterizing the phenomenon, with special emphasis on its peculiar manifestations in Latin America; second, a description of the Christian attitude toward this process; finally, a projection of that setting onto the structures of the Christian community in an effort to understand how they are conditioned by secularization and what the response to it should be.

A set of different phenomena have attracted the attention of sociologists, educators, historians, politicians, philosophers, theologians, and other scholars in the humanities and social sciences, prompting various studies that are converging from many different angles on some points of great

---

This chapter is based on the report of the commission on "Christian Community Structures and the Process of Secularization."

importance for understanding contemporary culture. There
has been much discussion of the "authority crisis," of "the
generation gap," and of "the weakening of traditional nuclei
which provided the standards for values and decisions in
human life," etc. At the same time human life has won
greater autonomy in decision making, granting greater freedom in social relations to those who live in situations of
insecurity and risk.

In one sense these phenomena are bound up in progressive secularization. This process, whose roots can be traced
to the close of the Middle Ages, has been gaining momen-
tum since the industrial revolution and is now beginning to
produce greater human maturity. As a result, the man of
our times is acquiring a more realistic outlook on his place
in the world and his relation to nature than ever before.
This process, then, offers enormous possibilities for human
existence as it simultaneously frees the individual from a
number of limitations and enables him to realize his privileged position within history as an essential element in
its development. It is important, therefore, for us to look
at some characteristics which can help us to understand
the process.

Secularization is universal, originating in the Christian
West. It has spread mainly through the extension and trans-
plantation of Western value concepts throughout the world,
accelerated in the last century thanks to the impact of scientific and technological development. So man has been
passing from a position of servitude to or struggle with
nature to a mastery which frees him for personal development (although, of course, this development has not pro-
gressed equally everywhere).

With the advance and dissemination of science the notions of the world which stemmed from a priori concepts re-
stricting the human being and his understanding of his

place in history and creation are progressively being abandoned or left behind. As a result, man is in a better position to understand his own fundamentally historical nature.

Another consequence of the process is the demise of the traditional metaphysical world view; in other words, reality is no longer apprehended from an absolute perspective. One must start with the facts as they appear. This perspective is simultaneously producing a widespread loss of interest in the traditional religious problems which once disturbed the human spirit and also leading to a renewed emphasis on history and everyday problems. Religious indifference and disinterest in the spiritual problems that formerly troubled man so greatly are steadily gaining ground and imposing themselves by means of secularization.

Looking at the problem from a more academic standpoint for the sake of accuracy and precision, the following may be given as historical facts: Even though, beginning in the thirteenth century, attacks were being directed against the system dominating medieval European society through a coalition of the church and the empire, Christendom did not begin to collapse until the breakup of European homogeneity in the sixteenth century. This weakening of Western Christianity became more evident with the barbarous religious wars which devastated Europe at the beginning of the seventeenth century, alienating large numbers of men from religious practice and dealing a great blow to the prestige of institutionalized religion. Official Christianity, in turn, trying to preserve its privileges, turned to reactionary groups, provoking the suppressed hostility among the masses. So it is not strange that when these groups were overthrown, Christianity also lost its direct access to the centers of power in most of the Western nations, a fact which becomes obvious in the nineteenth century. Accordingly, Christendom as "Christian society" is gone, and it is no longer possible to impose a Christian order on the social structure from the top. Most countries have instituted the separation of church and state, relegating religion to the sphere of private life.

To speak of secularization from a sociological viewpoint is to enumerate social changes. The decline of tradition and the greater autonomous decision-making power which modern man has acquired as secularization gains impetus are leading to the destruction of the traditional sacred foundations of society. Religion has borne the brunt of the impact; it has been relegated to increasingly restricted areas, contradicting its claim to be all-encompassing and to pronounce edicts binding all men. In addition, a similar process leading to the same results can be seen in the field of human consciousness. As human reason was freed from inhibiting religious and/or metaphysical presuppositions by means of self-critical analysis (Kant), the scientific and philosophical understanding of the world and man never fell back on elements beyond the scope of the scientific method. Consequently, God no longer has a place in either philosophy or the sciences, not even as a working hypothesis to help us understand the world.

The current result of this process is man's growing awareness of his place in the world, of his responsibility and his dignity. It necessitates a plan of action for full participation in the historical environment through which man may improve conditions for himself and society.

There is also a theological understanding of secularization as a process arising out of the preeminence of the activity of God in biblical history, which may be described as a process of desacralizing. From the standpoint of sociology and of the phenomenology of religion, the differentiation of the sacred and the profane constitutes the basis of man's religious activity. The sacred, according to the now classical formula of Rudolf Otto, is in essence the numinous, which is fascinating and alluring (*mysterium fascinans*) on the one hand, and repelling and terrifying (*mysterium tremens*) on the other. There is established, then, an essential dichotomy of being: consecrated cultic objects and the things of daily life, feast days and fast days, men entrusted with holy functions and those in charge of common worldly tasks, etc. Thus, the sacralizing of objects arises from the relationship established between them and the divinity or the sacred. Desacralizing, in turn, takes place when it is demonstrated that such sacralizings and even the sacred element itself are merely projections of the human spirit.

In the Bible, this desacralizing is intimately connected with the facts of the revelation of God, since these are diametrically opposed to understanding the action of the pagan gods of nature. In the natural religions the gods proffer an archetypal model of life emanating from their situation in a suprahistorical world of essences where change, time, and death do not exist. Or the natural religions may simply propose the elimination of the historical element, since man's action is irrevocably determined according to cycles fixed by that magical archetypal time. In contrast, the biblical witness points to something entirely different. In the Old Testament, God elects a people descended from a nomad in order to show the way proposed by God for the rest of the nations. This God enters into direct contact with men and acts through historical nations such as Assyria, Babylonia, Persia, etc., as well as through individuals who do not belong to the people of Israel, such as Nebuchadnezzar (cf. Jer. 43:10) or Cyrus (cf. Isa. 44:28 and 45:1). An important point is that his presence is not limited to holy places, and whenever it is assumed that he can only reveal himself in these, he intervenes to refute the assumption. Not even the temple, the center of worship, elicits special favor, undoubtedly because it has been transformed into an unwarranted source of security for a people who fail to realize that God's free presence is determined only by his sovereign will.

It is in Jesus Christ that this work of desacralizing is fully disclosed. Born of woman, in a manger, amid the prevailing poverty (Luke 2:1-7), he lived the life of the ordinary man: He was neither a Levite nor a scribe nor a "man of religion" according to the fashion of his day (Luke 4:20-24). When the moment arrived for him to take up his calling, he did not go off to the holy places but fulfilled his mission in the midst of society (Mark 1:14, Luke 4:14, Matt. 4:12-17) facing all the inherent risks. He broke down the Pharisaic legalism (Mark 2:23-28, Luke 13:10-17, etc.); he approached those scorned by the religious men of the day for their impious lives in order to include them in his group of disciples (Matt. 9:9-13). Once having formed his group of disciples, he demonstrated his lordship by washing their feet (John 13:1-24), concluding his life in shameful death on the cross between two thieves like any delinquent in his day (Mark 15:16-28 and parallel passages). This process of the full incarnation of God in man, mercifully redeeming the distance between divinity and humanity, between what could be regarded as sacred and what consequently becomes profane, is the final proof that God does not will any form of sacralizing. On the contrary, the God of the Bible is *holy* (Isa. 6:3), and so also are those whom he has elected (1 Cor. 1:2, Col. 1:2, etc.). The important thing to remember is that in the Bible *holiness* means a calling to fulfill a mission (1 Cor. 6:2). Or perhaps holiness cannot be understood without its operation in the world; not without reason *apostle* signifies one sent, that is, one sent into the world. The early Christian communities of the New

Testament understood this fact so well that the trusts created as offices in the church of the first century were designated by current terms from domestic rather than religious life (bishops *epískopos,* deacons *diákonos,* etc.). It follows that the perspective which emerges from the biblical message in reflecting upon desacralizing by means of the revelation of God offers no reason for resisting secularization but rather for bringing about a responsible openness to it.

Nevertheless, our understanding of secularization would be incomplete without a reminder of its intrinsically ambiguous nature. Clearly secularization, just as any other historical process, is not limited to only one meaning. Thus as it frees man from certain limitations that inhibit his full development, it creates others; for example, as religion continues losing its influence and prestige, certain current ideologies take on these attributes in such a way that, according to the canons of religious phenomenology, they may actually be defined as religious. Such is the case of the political devotion to certain charismatic personalities (a term designating extraordinary worth, charm, genius, or personality, with authority or power based on direct personal loyalty from followers in contrast with traditional or legal control, in which the personal element has been replaced by the institutional) or the complete obedience exacted by some totalitarian parties.

At the same time, it is important to distinguish between secularization and *secularism.* The latter appears when it is felt that the meaning of the process itself should be affirmed as the ultimate and definitive goal of history. Thus, from a particular (therefore conditioned and relative) observation of reality, a principle is inferred that claims to offer a complete comprehension of all of that reality. In this case, going beyond its bounds, secularism becomes a new metaphysical theory that, in virtue of the impossibility of confirming its assertions, distorts the facts.

Then again, secularization cannot always clearly effect the results mentioned before. In some cases, closely related to the historical conditions, its present appearance does not permit us to speak of the complete liberation of man or of the total abandonment of religion. Nevertheless, insofar as it is offering greater opportunities for the definition of a free and responsible personhood, its presence can be detected even in this characteristic ambivalence. It is appropriate, therefore, to speak of different stages reached during secularization.

In Latin America the process is not uniform. While in some regions a high degree of secularization predominates (the Río de la Plata area, Mexico, Cuba since the revolution, and the intellectual elite of every country), in others the process is being accelerated by contingent factors such as the skyrocketing urbanization which is rocking the continent. Or again, in conjunction with other perspectives, it has recently been unleashed, thanks to the influence of public education, technology, or science. So in spite of the fact that secularization is appearing in every sphere of human existence, in this case it is best to refer only to the religious aspect. Furthermore, it is imperative that we not forget the ambiguity in secularization since only thus can we understand the persistence of certain religious attitudes and styles of life alongside the results of a deep impression made by the process. In presenting the different levels attained by secularization in its impact on Latin American society and culture, we must point out that it is impossible to do justice to all the situations which secularization has brought about. Consequently, the following presentation will be schematic and therefore incomplete as deemed necessary for the sake of clarity in the exposition.

Secularization of the magical concept of the world indicates abandonment of a cosmic vision typical of the primitive mentality, in which the individual procured a relationship of familiarity and benevolence with the mysterious forces ruling the universe by participating in ritual or sacred acts which somehow enabled him to enter into communion with the elemental forces and in some cases win their favor in his behalf. At this level the desacralizing and demythologizing role of the gospel makes clear its power of secularization: With the command to worship God as the one true Lord who alone calls forth blessings for man (John 3:16), the world of phantasms, demons, and the forces of darkness is relegated to a less important position. Although that realm tends to remain on the Latin American scene, its influence is steadily diminishing.

From another standpoint, this liberation of man from the limitations of the mythical world view entails certain new responsibilities which he had disregarded because, as he understood it, mere man could not influence the course of events which ultimately awaited the meaning imposed on them by the underlying forces of life. In contrast, when a man feels called to act for the good of his neighbor, he becomes aware of his own authenticity and strives to be true to himself, which is a sign of responsibility.

It must be added that this secularization of the magical world is often a consequence of introducing science and/or technology into primitive communities; although this alone does not produce full secularization, it permits a greater development of human possibilities since many taboos are dropped when man recognizes his capacity for dominion over nature which formerly seemed hostile toward him.

Social change radically affects the value concepts and behavioral attitudes which characterize a traditional society.

The once-functional power centers decline. So it is with the traditional norms as well as the irrational elements which determine the style of life of such a society (honor, blood, social heritage, etc.). Just as man adopts specialized functions as a result of social change, religion also—which tended in traditional society to engulf all aspects of life— is relegated to a more specific and specialized realm, with a consequent loss of influence over the individual and society.

It has already been noted that the impact of social change does not always indicate the same degree of secularization. In many cases the masses who have converged on the central cities in the urbanization process have been challenged by the society to adopt a new way of life, but in any case they also continue to maintain the values and standards corresponding to the traditional society. It is proper at this point to mention the danger of rootlessness which in some instances leads to situations of social anomie. In this case, the manifestation of secularization may well mean the abandonment not of all forms of religious life, but of those pertaining to traditional society, replaced by others consonant with the new social configuration. Such is the case of the upsurge of spiritualism in Brazil, especially in the Sao Paulo area. The task is then to create a world view based not on a primordial religious stance nor on adherence to certain religious creeds deemed essential for man, but rather on religious thinking that emerges from the context of man's new situation.

One factor promoting secularization among its adherents is the Marxist ideology. While religion is promoting otherworldliness and human behavior according to transcendental requisites, Marxism is offering itself to the Latin American masses as a useful instrument in facing the grave problems of daily life that assail the less fortunate classes and as a means of fighting for a more just society. With regard to this last aspect of secularization one must not overlook its ambiguity and dangers, for the known socialist societies also create restrictions and forms of alienation which hinder the full development of man. Even though Marxism encourages atheism, it can also betray the meaning of secularization, as has occurred in places by way of sacralizing structures, ideological positions, and even personalities.

The theme of a mature culture has already been mentioned in reference to some results of secularization. This aspect is especially dear to intellectual circles in Latin America and tends to expand among those reaching a high level of intellectual attainment. Such a culture is the effect of the development of human character which, even as it demands eradication of all restraining barriers, insists on the importance of observation and criticism in the field of knowledge. Consequently, there are no longer any topics which cannot come under examination and investigation. With this comes perseverance not only in the destruction of taboos and the demystification of a world view out of touch with reality but also in the further evolution of man and society.

Regretting the inability to go into detail, we must simply present the most typical attitudes produced in the Christian community in response to secularization. As in preceding paragraphs, the exposition of this point will be done schematically, recognizing once again the dangers inherent in such a procedure, especially since such attitudes never appear in perfectly pure forms.

The attitude of rejection need not be described, but it is important to consider the reasons behind it. One of the basic motivations for this attitude is fear of any change. As is well known, the process of change casts doubt upon the firm bases which for a long time have supported human existence and social living. For one thing, this fear results from ignorance of what the changes may bring. This fear of social change appears, however, in those groups or institutions which have enjoyed privileges and/or authority and are afraid of losing them in the process. This is true of many traditional churches and some religious institutions which assume a defensive attitude of rejection in the face of change. In these instances it is a matter of reaction motivated by fear of losing the traditional *status* of religion.

Another motivation for rejection is the fear of loss of control, not in the authority of religion but in the actual forms of religious life and their appropriate symbols. In the life style of a traditional society religion occupies a central place. When, however, it is removed to more limited, peripheral, and confining quarters, it reacts against the decline of religious practice or religious following, condemning the process that has caused this new situation.

Just as there are groups who reject change for the insecurity it engenders, there are also those who accept it or emphasize it. There are several possible motives such as dilettantism of change, the attitude of uncritical receptivity to all forms of all social change, and frustration over the anachronism of many forms of Christian life. In the latter case, the urgent need for adapting to secularization, arrested by adherence to traditional forms of expression, determines the abandonment of the traditional forms and the full and free acceptance of conditions imposed by the new situation. Another more profound motive arises from taking into account only the positive aspects of secularization, ignoring the opposite elements which also belong to the ambiguous picture. This position, like the two preceding, fails to recognize the relative and absolute aspects of every historical phenomenon.

Finally we must realize that for many Christians the unfolding of the process is so evident, the consequences so inevitable, that—abandoning any possibility for responsible study—they think it is only a question of adjusting to the process. In this instance, renewal of the forms of Christian life, personal and communal, can emerge not from an act of communal reflection followed by truly authentic projection, but from an updating in the face of events.

The phrase "responsible involvement in the process" is intended to characterize the attitude of those who—having forsaken the role of spectators, relinquished all dogmatic positions based on a priori elements not borne out by the actual facts, and rejected any precipitate commitment to the process—become responsibly involved in it in such a way as to keep open the possibilities for greater human development as the situation allows. This approach seriously considers all that the process entails in order to enter into the events that constitute it, contriving to shape them in the interests of man in his totality. This responsible involvement cannot be based on theoretical positions; rather, it is authentic solely to the degree of its participation in the actual events.

Responsible involvement issues from awareness of the unfolding of the process, which implies not necessarily an evaluation (negative or positive) of it, but a serious examination of all its implications and possibilities. Responsible involvement is the immediate consequence already implicit in the point of departure of this attitude. Furthermore, it means paying closer attention to what is happening in secular history, discerning the activity of God in the midst of events, and inviting others to share in it.

The foregoing gives rise to a search for new modes of expression and new structures in the Christian community. At this point one must again recall the repeatedly emphasized ambiguity of secularization as well as of any given historical situation. Even though the thrust of the Bible and the facts of history call for acceptance of the secular, one must not forget that it can also be accomplished dialectically by means of religious elements which in turn must be secularized. For this very reason it is impossible absolutely to demand a secularization of the forms of Christian life. All that can be said is that traditional ways, distorted in many respects by the negative aspects of religion (which secularization is rendering as anachronistic expressions of life and relegating to less important levels), can become a deterrent to the Christian community wishing to face the new situation responsibly. The structures of the community of believers in Christ should be readily adaptable to the action of God in history (cf. chapters two and three of this book). Such a position would soon lead to a careful examination of the problem of Christian communal structures. First, however, it would be wise to clarify the difference between faith and religion.

Reference has been made in this chapter to the negative aspect of religion. This attitude is not primarily the result of secularization, but it is most clearly rooted in the Bible. We have seen how the God of biblical revelation stands over against the gods of the religions: Others worship idols shaped by the hands or spirit of men (Ps. 96:5). In contrast, the God of revelation, the living God, "the God of Abraham, Isaac, and Jacob," prevails over these gods, since he is in no way a projection of human desires: thence the reaction of Yahweh in Exodus 32:7-10 to the building of the golden calf by the people waiting at the foot of Mt. Sinai. The attitude demanded by the God of the Bible is not religion (a complex of beliefs, ceremonies, sacrifices, laws to fulfill, and restrictions to observe), but faith (Hos. 6:6, Matt. 9:13, Amos 5:21-23, etc.).

Religion thus appears to be a complex of acts through which man is able to approach and commune with divinity, but which, on the other hand, is no more than the projection of his sublimated ideal of humanity, community, or nation. Man projects his drives onto an order which he believes to be eternal. This order, holding him in subjection, becomes a curb to his desire for expansion, vitality, and freedom. The most important thing for the religious man is to share in that eternal order; consequently, any threat against that realm is dangerous—is an attack on the taboo —and if the taboo is broken down, chaos may result. In this context religion is a true factor in the alienation of man: It diverts him from everyday life and keeps him from becoming master of his own life, responsible for himself and able to define humanity in his own terms.

Faith, on the other hand, appears to be response to God (Rom. 10:17), to revelation. As such, faith is a human act, arising not from the initiative of the individual but in his response to the divine act. God reveals himself in modes appropriate to man, that is, through history. At the same time, faith demands responsibility to one's neighbor since "he who does not love his brother whom he has seen, cannot love God whom he has not seen" (1 John 4:20), or as expressed in the preceding verse, "We love, because he first loved us." Likewise, the parable of the Good Samaritan and Jesus' teaching on the last judgment (Matt. 25:31-46) indicate that faith is response to the love of God, manifested in love of one's neighbor.

Nevertheless, we must continue to stress the fact that faith has very seldom in the course of history been realized in such a pure and simple form. It stands to reason that the Christian attitude which gave rise to religion was derived from the faith of the first disciples; in the same way, the people of Israel turned the faith of the patriarchs into a religion, which the prophets opposed. The important thing is that by the demand of the gospel, the Christian community came again and again to reform the exercise of its faith in order to preserve its character of response to the act of God, an act which contains the force of a binding engagement with the concrete historical situations in which it is participating. Faith, as response to the revelation of God in history (as is the case with the God of the Bible), demands real commitment to and involvement in the course of human events. There can be no escape from the scene of action nor retreat to the realm of inwardness. Although there, too, God may be at work, the presence and action of the Holy Spirit make it imperative for the man of faith to be constantly in the thick of events. Recall, for instance, Paul's insistence on going to Jerusalem in spite of the dangers awaiting him and his later insistence on being judged as a Roman citizen, which resulted in his journey to Rome. Again and again, faith demanded his presence in the crux of the situation, not an escape to the sidelines. In such a context, acting out of complete responsibility, filled with love, the man of faith shall proclaim new patterns for humanity in token of the coming kingdom or the presence of God. Ultimately, though the world may wish to ignore those signs and that presence, ". . . faith is the assurance of things hoped for, the conviction of things not seen" (Heb. 11:1).

As has been said, secularization and its impact on culture and society have directly affected the community of believers. Accordingly, in the course of social transition and its repercussions, Christians keep asking themselves what constitutes Christian action and what type of organization or structures can make it more viable and apparent for nonbelievers. In response to these questions we shall follow this procedure: first, an examination of several sociological elements of the Christian community; second, a probe of the New Testament for certain basic statements about the life of some Christian communities in that time; finally, an attempt at dialogue between theology and sociology concerning the nature of the church.

The Christian community lives today in a very singular situation, characterized in Latin America by the rise of numerous urban and industrial centers. In this new situation religion has lost its place in important policy-making decisions, and its traditional social functions have been taken over by new centers of power, interest, and influence. There is also a growing crisis over the traditional concept of authority. In another quarter specialization is becoming more intensified in the various customary fields. New types of associations based not on geographical locale (neighborhood, township, parish), but on functional sectors of society, are appearing.

The Christian community, however, continues to maintain an ecclesiastical structure which conformed to an administrative framework and church organization imported from abroad but which present experience has now proved inadequate in the changing circumstances of Latin America. Furthermore, the Christian community seems unconscious of the impact of the crisis of social change on the institutional level; thus it continues operating within traditional moulds in a new social situation (which accounts for their inadequacy). At the same time the church assumes an authority relevant to the past but now anachronistic, at least in the areas where social change has been and is underway.

The classical congregational or parochial structure of the Christian community is accordingly out of tune with the urban situation. Circumstances demand the exercise of great freedom of action, possible only in a highly flexible and dynamic congregational organization. This has been blocked by, among other things, the so-called "edifice complex" which in many cases has reached the point of sacralizing a special place (temple) which comes to be considered indispensable for the life, worship, and existence of the community of believers, thus obscuring the vision of the life and mission of the church.

In other cases it may be that stratification and division by sex and/or age of the members of the congregation, whether in Sunday schools or inner circles of the local congregation, reveal the increasingly anachronistic nature of their structures. This is so because such factors are scarcely related to the real sweep of interests and occupations in the modern emergent society of Latin America, which seems to indicate that the Christian community is not doing full justice to the concerns, aspirations, anxieties, and conditioning forces of contemporary Latin American man.

In the typical rural-traditional society the Christian community was the nerve center of social life; however, preserving old structures means entering into an ineffectual and ill-advised competition with secular organizations that perform more effectively than the Christian community various cultural, social, and recreational functions. The most important reason, however, for the church to abandon these functions is based on the fact that the Christian community should never duplicate natural social structures but should pervade them so that there its members may have the opportunity to serve and witness.

The classical type of pastorate in the Christian community of Latin America is all-embracing and determinative, tending to subsume all the roles appropriate to the traditional social leader. As can be seen, there is no consideration of the fact that the Christian community draws on personal resources from the different professional fields, members who can perform within the congregation the special functions consonant with their respective vocations.

The New Testament offers us an image of the people of God at once extremely dynamic and highly flexible with regard to structures. Those of the congregation at Corinth (cf. 1 Cor. 12) are not the same as those outlined in the letter to the Romans (Rom. 12:6-8) nor those appearing in the letter to the Ephesians (Eph. 4:1-16). A probe into the pastoral epistles discloses that the bishop has been carrying out several ministries previously performed by various members of the congregation (cf. especially 1 and 2 Tim.). In the light of that structural flexibility in the early Christian congregations, there arises the possibility (and even necessity) for the Christian community to be constantly revising its structures in light of the biblical message.

The Christian community is called to fulfill a specific vocation at each juncture, responding to the specific challenges presented. Unfortunately, in the face of social change and under the impact of secularization, the Christian congregation appears in many instances resolute in its stance of rejection. Therefore, the prime requisite for the Christian community is always to express anew, with relevance to the current situation, the totality of the new life in Christ. This does not imply the repudiation of given factors in the social reality but rather their transformation, requiring first a serious assessment of all the implications.

The New Testament image of the Christian community as the human group in which are manifest the "first fruits of the kingdom" and the "new humanity" is of obvious importance. That truth can be realized only to the extent that the structural framework makes possible the new creation in Christ, the breaking forth of a richer and more human society. In pursuit of that structure the Christian com-

munity must first rid itself of all the dead weight that prevents it from witnessing to the fact that God is bringing
about the creation of the world and that this work of
creation is, above all, the redemption of man. Only then
will the message proclaimed cease to be just a verbal sign
and become the living word incarnate.

The example of Jesus Christ, denying himself, relinquish-
ing his divinity and taking the form of the servant (*doulos*:
slave), is normative for the structures of Christian community and the organization of its ministry. The form of
the servant permits Jesus Christ to be present among men
and truly serve them (Phil. 2:5-11). Those who belong to
the Christian community must therefore be "in full accord
and of one mind" (Phil. 2:2), the mind which is in Christ
Jesus (Phil. 2:5); this may be translated as assuming the
form of the servant as a sign of the service of Jesus Christ
in and for the world.

According to the New Testament the Christian community is a body of ministers called to express themselves
in terms of service. It follows that their new communal
structure must abandon all claims to prestige or to statisti-
cal success; it should be identified by the requirements of
service and witness in relation to problems generated and
conditioned by actual concrete situations.

As previously stated, the Christian community should
demonstrate a way of life characterized by responsible and
loving service to men; this is the sign of "the first fruits of
the new life." Its formal structures should promote, not
hinder, this service. Applying this to the wide range of circumstances of Christian congregations, it is easy to see that
there can be no absolute structures; rather, they must be
dynamic and flexible in order to express in ever new forms
the event of faith and the encounter of men with Jesus
Christ. It is therefore necessary to consider the tension be-

tween the structural organization, which may be geared to the life and mission of the Christian community, and the actual state of that community in its visible manifestations. Such tension may be resolved in several ways.

In many cases it is resolved in favor of those who reject any movement pressing for revision of congregational structures. Hence there prevails a dogmatic attitude which sees the present organization of the Christian community as definitive, ignoring the precarious element inherent in every human organization, including the Christian community insofar as it is an institution. Others repudiate everything implied by institutions. Consequently, they tend to express themselves in constantly changing and dynamic forms, thus avoiding any type of institutionalism and emphasizing the sense of motion in the community.

Neither of these responses takes into account all the implications of the factors mentioned. The rejectionist attitude, for its part, forgets that the Christian community is an historical institution which has evolved over the centuries as the history of the church clearly shows. Even in their dynamic fervor, those wishing to avoid any form of institutional life whatsoever cannot escape some institutional design, since even constant change represents in a certain sense the institutionalization of action by which the life of the Christian community may be directed.

Considering all the implications of the incarnation of God in Jesus Christ as the vicarious servant of mankind, one conclusion is that the Christian community must be organized for human expression. Therefore, there can be no categorical rejection of institutions since every human group which purports to perform a function in history must of necessity organize itself, thus establishing some inevitable institutional rules.

The important question is what type of organization we

are dealing with. Let us recall some previous points: The Christian community should structure itself not rigidly nor definitively (in such case, it would be rejecting its own historicity and the historical changes that condition it, leading ultimately to denying the incarnation of the Word), but dynamically and flexibly, allowing for spontaneity in its manifestations. In this way it could effectually express itself as a community in the midst of historical events as well as the servant of men participating in the transformation of society. Such structural freedom together with creative spontaneity will be clear signs of authenticity and vitality.

The problem of the organization that shapes the life of the Christian community leads us to consider the relationships between the Holy Spirit and the church. In the book of Acts these relationships are described in highly dynamic terms: It is the Holy Spirit who constantly challenges the community with possibilities for action in concrete situations, in the face of which the group of believers acts responsibly, accepting the particular challenge proffered by the Holy Spirit (cf. the day of Pentecost: Acts 2; the baptism of the Gentiles in the home of Cornelius: Acts 10; the baptism of a eunuch by Philip: Acts 8:26-40; the "Come over to Macedonia and help us," demanding of Paul a reply, which, being affirmative, signalled the beginning of the evangelization of Europe: Acts 16:9 f.). The Holy Spirit guides the Christian community, not by mysterious and incomprehensible inspirations, but rather by means of challenges embodied in particular historical situations.

If this is applied to the problem at hand, it follows that the Christian community must develop structures which will permit real openness to the exigencies of historical events and encourage the serious exercise of responsibility in light of the work of the Holy Spirit. In this way the community structures will lend themselves to the actualization of faith and encounter (although it is understood that ultimately this depends not on human structures, but on the will of God). In other words, the structures should grant sufficient liberty that through them the Christian community may give birth to and manifest the character of the new humanity which God is creating through his action in history. It follows that one should beware of the danger of sacralizing the new structures, always remembering to treat them as functional and transitory.

Finally, we suggest some specific situations which should be kept in mind as guidelines for structural change within the actual Latin American context. The search for structural renewal, involving some Latin American churches under the pressure of urgent demands for change, implies not only local organizational revision but coordinated national reformation of church structures.[1] New experiences have led the local congregation to become the focal point of community life where it has directed community organization among and in service to socially marginal groups. Developments are occuring through the mergence of such organizations as the Student Christian Movement and the Church and Society groups, which—while not actually church institutions (even though they constitute vanguard movements in the life of the Christian community)—are fitting instruments for church renewal. Experiments with "vanguard groups" placed in dialogue and permanent confrontation with the world may give rise to new theological developments. These groups should work out for themselves functional forms of organization bearing in mind the following criteria:

Certain spots and geographical areas in Latin America are in urgent need of such groups. Even more important in the secular society are the human zones (vocational, professional, and functional groups characteristic of modern society) which present themselves as fields for specific forms of Christian witness: universities, labor unions, political circles, young people's organizations, neighborhood groups. In the organization of these ventures the participation of specialists and other committed persons should be in keeping with the nature of the project. For the sake of coordination these groups should keep in close contact with those of a similar design even when they are working in different fields. Assuming their eventual ecumenical integration, these groups should be assisting one another for the sake of community advancement by seeking out new dimensions of the gospel, the symbols of Christian life, the means of grace, and the sacraments.

---

1. The Presbyterian Reformed Church of Cuba, for example, is facing a new experience which requires the formation of a National Legislative Assembly and three Provincial Assemblies to execute its projects, which are designed for simplicity, efficiency, and greater lay participation in the life of the church. The national body will have a functional present-oriented structure, maintaining sufficient flexibility to avoid becoming a "sacred block" impervious to future change.

6

Faith, Ideology, and Social Justice

Ideology and Faith in a Rapidly Changing Society

Faith is personal response to the word of God revealed in Jesus Christ, which addresses man in the midst of his historical situation through the inspiration of the Holy Spirit. Ideologies are theoretical concepts of reality, conditioned by the historical situation (economic, social, cultural) of the groups which hold them, aiding such groups in planning their course of action so as to achieve and uphold their goals.

Despite the proximity of the two definitions, their distance becomes apparent when they are set against the background in which each has been formulated: theology, in the case of faith; the social sciences, in the case of ideology. The objective conditions contributive to faith are always present at every moment in history, because God is always the same even though his answers, in accordance with their existential nature, vary with historical circumstances. The objective conditions for ideologies, on the other hand, correspond to a definite historical situation, perish with it, and do not recur, thus giving every ideology its necessarily contingent nature. Nevertheless, both faith and ideologies operate in the common realm of time and space: in history.

This chapter is based on the reports of the committees on "Ideology and Faith in a Rapidly Changing Society" and "Social Justice and the Traditional Society."

Faith, response to God, requires encounter with one's neighbor in the concrete situation. One's neighbor is the needy, the least significant, the poorest (Matt. 25:31-45); wherever he is found in a situation of structural poverty (poverty determined not by personal inadequacy, but by the encompassing social structures), faith demands social action to deliver him from that poverty by changing not simply his individual situation, but the social framework responsible for it. In the urgency of that demand for social action the Christian faces an ideological option between various models for his course of action (Amos 5:4-20). The Christian cannot make this decision on the basis of a philosophy of history, a world view, a system of ideas, a set of principles, humanism (whether "Christian" or not), or any other ideology ("Christian" or otherwise).

The ideological choice must be made on the basis of the word of God to his people (Heb. 1:1-4), beginning with it and in constant reference to it as the only supreme norm, in connection with a theology of history clearly informed by the human situation, described and understood according to the methodology of the social sciences. Essential to this theology of history is a Christology which affirms Jesus (the historical person) as Christ (the Messiah), Son of God and Son of man, the Risen One who is to come. Without constant personal reference to the person of Christ as Lord of history, Christian faith becomes ideology.

This personal relationship with Jesus Christ must recognize in him the risen Lord who personally calls man in the here and now to answer responsibly in relation to God and to his neighbor (not only to his brother) in that historical juncture. Moreover, it must also recognize in him the One who is to come, who is to judge all men according to their action or inaction toward each of the needy ones (Luke 10:15-37), and who today urges an attitude of *watchfulness* in expectation of the sudden arrival of the day of our Lord Jesus Christ; of *courage* magnified to the utmost; of *mission,* proclaiming the gospel to all men; of *action,* serving the poor in concrete acts which in this historical juncture must necessarily be a revolutionary task (Matt. 24-25).

As we then emphatically affirm the duty of the Christian to adopt an ideology of change, one fundamental question remains: Can the same ideological choice be exacted of a Christian community, of a denomination of the church? We realize that lack of ecclesiastical consensus in Latin American Protestantism makes an answer impossible at this time; nevertheless, it is clear that theological investigation through an ecumenical inquiry is imperative.

In accordance with the definition of ideology posited in the beginning, we here refrain from making a classification of ideologies which would generalize the situation throughout the hemisphere and consequently disregard the individuality of each country according to the peculiarities of its development. Church and Society in Latin America must therefore encourage regional and national studies of each particular ideological complex; toward this end, we make the following general recommendations.

First it will be necessary to establish a typology of the principal ideologies with their main branches, subtypes, and derivatives, to serve as the frame of reference for regional empirical studies and subsequently to be revised in light of these findings.

In studying a situation, one should keep in mind the historical development of each ideology and its assimilation or rejection in the course of economic changes, social struggles, and modifications of the power structure.

In the light of these interrelations, one should examine the conservative or transformative tendency of each ideology, its political efficacy, and its influence on the masses. In any society where there is an ideological void due to the inadequacy or lack of appeal of existing ideologies, the causes and possible solutions of this problem must be investigated.

In this study one must always remember the crucial role of ideologies in eliciting popular participation. We cannot accept the prediction of the end of ideologies, at least not with reference to Latin America; this assertion is attributable to certain sectors who trust exclusively in technological development to improve conditions without severe social problems. In our situation this attitude deters the push for transformation of the class structures and thus constitutes a force for preserving the status quo.

In analyzing an ideological complex, it is profitable first to distinguish the ideologies supporting the existing system from those wishing to change it. Among the former set one will discover fine differences, even to the extent of some meager notions of modifying the prevailing system; in the great majority of cases, however, one will find a common laissez-faire liberal persuasion. The most important task is to determine their positions within the general framework of this liberalism and, as far as possible, their relations with other variations of this current in the contemporary world: developmentalism, "gorilismo" (repressive military control), etc.

With no pretensions of establishing a rigorous classification for all situations, we may differentiate among the ideologies of social change, those of international scope, and those of national origin. Of the first type, Marxism and the widening gap among Communist parties along the lines of Soviet and non-Soviet orientation merit special attention. Among those groups designated "Christian," one will find Christian Democratic parties, Christian Socialist parties, and others.

Most of all, the national popular movements require

local individualized study. As they have been born in different countries at different historical junctures with almost
no reference to the major international ideologies, they
should be interpreted as outgrowths of their own historical
environments. Nevertheless, it is possible to delineate similarities among groups which shed light upon each other,
showing the relationship among movements such as those
under the name of Perón in Argentina, Vargas in Brazil,
Aprismo in Peru, etc., but respecting their different moments
and connections with other ideologies. On occasion the research must become highly specific, since the fault of some
of these movements lies precisely in their ideological in-
consistency, often substituted by the appeal of a charismatic
personality. Nevertheless, these personalities, over and above
the mere emotional response, create among the masses ideological attitudes and a certain minimum of common ideas.

In conclusion it should be noted that the ideological
moment of Latin America coincides with an accelerated
process of secularization, which does not advance uniformly
or straightforwardly but varies in stage and form from one
region to another. On this ground it becomes possible to
speak of a single ideological outlook throughout Latin America; the basic fact common to all seems to be a mutual stance
in relation to secularization and our condition of dependence
within the international economic structure. That shared
viewpoint is the realization that man's duty is to enter
into this process, not as spectator but as actor, not as a
predetermined object but as a free subject determining his
future (Gen. 1:28).

Social Justice and the Traditional Society

From the biblical viewpoint, the just man is one who
does all that he should—all that he is called to do in a given
situation. The Bible offers no universally valid concept of

social justice by which to measure man's acts or perhaps God's action but clearly explains (particularly in the book of Amos) that every man is personally responsible for exercising justice toward others in his specific situation. In the context of God's covenant with man, justice means loyalty to the covenant, hence the specifically religious character of the biblical concept of justice: God's justice toward man and the justice of man toward God and his fellowmen.

Social justice acquires its meaning from this context; it is the justice of man toward other men. This is not equivalent to the ideal of human equality; rather, it is faithfulness to God, who has established and commanded justice among men. The prophetic denunciations of injustice are motivated not merely by social interests, but by religious concern. Justice is the right of the poor and the oppressed. It is the right of life or death which God holds over all men. In that sense historical life, especially the death and resurrection of Christ, is a verdict of God. His justice should be considered not as something apart, but as that historical judgment which has been pronounced. God has pronounced a judgment completely changing the condition of man and of the whole universe. Man, however, does not easily accept that change; he rebels against his new condition. Nevertheless, man is called by God to discover ways to show his justice, not by the mechanical application of a rule, but as the concrete symbol of the goodness and mercy of God toward his creatures. On this basis we are in a position today to struggle and toil so that God's justice may be seen in Latin America through our social justice, that is, through man's justice to man.

The conquest and colonization of Latin America principally by the Spanish and Portuguese led to imposing the forms of political and social organization and of the dominant religion in these nations with no regard for the patterns of government, land tenure and exploitation, or social customs and community organization of the primitive indigenous societies. The wealth of the land and the mines passed into the hands of the crown, and the *encomienda* (a regal grant including land and serfs) was adopted as the pattern of exploitation. The hacienda, which constitutes the socio-economic unit prevalent in most Latin American countries today, is heir to a large part of the basic organization of that *encomienda* system: great expanses of land in the hands of a single landowner and subsistence or subhuman living conditions for the vast numbers of workers. The hacienda thus became established as the basis of economic, political, and military power and determined the model of authority (the *hacendado* or landlord) still prevalent in most of the continent; here is the basic root of the political immaturity and dependency and the minimal participation in socio-economic affairs of the peasant and Indian sectors of Latin America.

As many historians have shown, political independence did not fundamentally alter the patterns of the colonial system. The authority of the king was succeeded by that of the creole aristocracy, and the dominant minority maintained its privileges and controls over the economic resources, consolidating the marked social imbalance. The streams of immigration opened up near the end of the last century initiated a steady urbanization trend, stimulated economic development, and introduced new political ideologies and other modernizing factors giving rise to the emergence of a middle class and a progression toward democratic forms of political and social life, especially in the urban areas.

In spite of these signs of social transformation, the cultural norms and pattern of authority inherited from the colonial systems still survive today in the rural sectors and have unexpectedly impinged upon the urban situation as a result of the two phenomena having greatest social impact on the life of the continent today: the population explosion and the waves of internal migration to the cities. The latter phenomenon has had very complex political consequences and may serve to explain the rise of a new type of Latin American dictator as in the cases of Perón in Argentina and Vargas in Brazil. Furthermore, the Latin American economic system has not undergone any fundamental alteration; the *latifundio* (possession of vast landholdings) continues to be the basic problem in landownership, and even the moderate industrial development which has occurred in various countries due to foreign capital and the control of the production means by a small minority has been unable to modify the social structure to the benefit of the masses.

The traditional society was conducive to a predominantly conservative mentality or ideology, identified with the socioeconomic system inherited from the colonial era and by the same token opposed to any social reform movement and even to the forces that impelled the continent toward its first urban and industrial development. Upheld by the traditional forces of the landowning class—the army and the ecclesiastical hierarchy—this conservative mentality managed to control political power and maintain the traditional status in the great majority of Latin American countries until very recent times.

In its time the independence movement had received its inspiration from the liberal and democratic ideas of the period, particularly those predominant in France and the United States. Many of the constitutions and legal systems of the Latin American nations followed the example of the United States. This new liberal current took root in the cities, spread democratic ideals in the fields of politics and education, and channeled the aspirations of the rising middle class, clashing with the conservative ideology and parties in the realm of politics. But even in the countries in which liberalism succeeded in imposing its concept of government and its democratic institutions, the dichotomy between the rural (conservative) and urban sectors persists today. This fact, however, is not presently of ultimate importance, owing to developments which have changed the face of the Latin American situation today.

The undeniable failure of the ideology and the economic and political organization of liberalism either to challenge effectively the interests of the conservative groups or to promote true social development in Latin America made inevitable the introduction and diffusion of new ideologies in which revolutionary concepts of political and social change and socialist forms of economic organization predominated. Marxism and its different political variants (socialism, communism, Trotskyism, anarchism) lay the groundwork for these ideologies and so opened the door to elements that radically transformed the political picture of the continent.

Along with the Marxist trends two other currents became identified with a concept of social change, espousing similar objectives. The first is revolutionary nationalism, a force with no coherent ideological expression but with great potentialities by virtue of its ability to galvanize vast sectors of the population (at times extracted from the traditional parties) on the bases of a certain mystique and the use of unifying symbols. Simultaneously certain intellectual circles and organizations gave birth to a current which had been spreading under the name of *desarrollismo* (developmentalism), based originally on several scientific studies of the Latin American situation. Its central feature is a "technocratic" concept of change, in which the factors of politics and popular involvement are sidestepped and the mission of transforming the socio-economic structure is entrusted to a group of technologists, in keeping with modernistic canons now in vogue.

The political scene has presently been modified significantly by the challenge of certain privileges and interests by these new ideologies, in some cases Marxist-oriented and in others decisively nationalist, and by their mobilization of the people in favor of radical changes. The conservative and liberal groups (through an alliance inconceivable a few decades ago) have succeeded in mobilizing the economic and military resources to consolidate the current political and economic structure and to postpone indefinitely the changes demanded by the masses and by the actual developmental needs of the continent. This effort has allied several traditional groups (the landowning class, the army) with the more recent industrial bourgeoisie, the bankers and foreign interests represented in Latin America by their important inventions and backed by the intervention of their own government and army (United States).

Faced with their situation and the inescapable task of seeking and proclaiming a concrete expression of the biblical concept of social justice, the church can do nothing less than define its message and its mission amid the political and social tensions which have arisen in Latin America. Four aspects of this mission seem fundamental: to proclaim the sovereignty of God over human relations and the whole of life; to point out the relativity and precariousness of every human institution, including national economic, political, and social structures, and the ultimate purpose for which they have been created—to serve man and thereby to glorify God; to offer an interpretation of the historical moment which the continent is experiencing, facing the judgment and the redemptive plan of God for man; to act as spokesman and defender of all victims of social injustice, pointing to its causes and agents.

For the execution of this task neither a pious life nor intensive communal activity will suffice. Through its members the church must be present in the front lines of the struggle for social justice. On many occasions the need for this presence and this active witness will lead Christians into the struggle beside those whom the church has traditionally considered its adversaries and who in turn have believed the church to be an instrument of oppression and domination by the powerful classes. Any such consideration which causes the Christian community to forget its principal mandate for social justice and the liberation of man may be, in the present historical situation, an act of disobedience toward the Lord. For only through an active pursuit, by nature risky and difficult, of justice as it is conceived in the Bible, can the church offer its witness and carry out God's mission for the redemption of man fulfilled once for all in Christ.

7

The Political Crisis in Latin America and Christian Participation

One of the signs of institutional crisis is the lack of correspondence between the formal juridical descriptions of the institutions and the empirical social reality. Analysis of political structures shows that political power (a) is not exercised, even indirectly, by the prescribed entities or groups through the formal legal and political structures ("the people"), so that we face a lack of representation and (b) is not even fully exercised by the limited sectors who appear to manage public affairs, owing to the phenomenon which should be classified "dependence on foreign groups" and which, in turn, comes under the broader category of economic and political "imperialism."

Our institutional framework is the product of liberalism, which instituted the State for the preservation of individual liberties. From the very beginning, however, this political doctrine contained grave contradictions which, in the course of time, came to undermine the whole structure. It tacitly presupposes the existence of private property to be defended against the attacks both of fellow citizens and likewise of the State. Consequently, it postulates an insuperable dichotomy between "liberty" and "equality." It operates on the assumption of an "equality of opportunities" for all men, which is, however, a mere formality; and it supposes that the sum

---

This chapter is based on the report of the committee on "Crisis and Revolution in Political Structures."

total of individual egoism (private initiative) will "naturally" add up to the good of the community. Its ethic is utilitarian, equating the operation of the state with that of private enterprise, of which the rationale is the amassing of profit without regard for the ultimate purposes of that profit for the benefit of the whole community. In the leading economic nations "equality of opportunities" for all, including groups that assume the forms of private initiative, has been nullified by the formation of monopolistic groups. At least in these cases the profits are reinvested and used to the advantage of a limited sector of the nation. The economically marginal nations, as we shall see, do not enjoy even this benefit.

Private accumulation of capital, the economic presupposition of liberalism, could not be realized in our societies, which served only as sources of such capital without ever enjoying the benefits. As a result, our societies suffer not only the current practical negation of the juridical form of liberal institutions but also an increasing economic deterioration.

The basic elements of the formal power structure as it appears in our legal ordinances reflect the general aspects of the liberal political doctrine: representative government and the balance of power among the executive, the legislative, and the judicial. At the time of its independence our continent lacked the fundamental economic premises which undergirded liberalism in Europe and the United States; this institutional framework was, therefore, imposed upon our constitutions as a model of the ideal society toward which one should aim, not as a political instrument for the well-being of society. Just as in other societies of liberal political origin, this legal order has actually come to consolidate the privileges of those who enjoyed the major benefit of the wealth of our countries; in our case, the situation is aggravated by the outflow of capital produced by such highly limited circles to other nations. This institutional framework has thus proved untenable even as fiction; its perpetual distortion is demonstrated in these days (1966) by the existence of six *de facto* governments, three dictatorships, and the continual instability among Latin American governments.

As is the case in economically strong societies of liberal political makeup, the centers of decision making are not those foreseen by the constitution. In our countries the groups making the real political and economic decisions are the traditional oligarchies—the new industrial bourgeoisie, the church, and the armed forces. The oligarchy, which has been direct heir to the Spanish colonial regime (regardless of successive changes of metropolises), has retained power until recent decades, even though in some countries it has had to yield to the middle class in the formal exercise of power. Nevertheless, even today it still controls many institutions, including the judiciary, the diplomatic apparatus, and a good measure of the mass communications media (especially the daily press). The source of wealth of these nuclei has been the possession of vast tracts of land and its exploitation in agriculture and cattle. Their style of life and system of values are not of the feudal type, as has sometimes been erroneously asserted, but are largely patterned after the North-Atlantic societies.

In analyzing the political crisis of our countries, we must strongly emphasize the dependence of the domestic power centers on foreign economic groups. Our first probe has led us to see that power is in fact not exercised by the agencies prescribed in our juridical systems. This is also the case in the highly developed nations of original liberal structure, but here the similarities end.

Furthermore, political decisions in our nations are made by extracontinental national groups. Precisely because the accumulation of the first capital dividends was never reinvested in our countries, their liberal structure was falsified from the beginning. Clearly then, even the domestic political decision-makers that one discovers in a first cursory analysis are not responsible for the final decisions. Even they are only intermediaries compelled to act in the interests of the great epicenters of international economics (metropolises). We face an imperialism which defends its economic interests through disguised political manipulation. The connecting links with the real centers of political power are not always easy to identify, with the exception of a limited number of regions in Latin America. Rather, they act through the intermediation of different pressure groups, which frequently give every appearance of being national. Nevertheless, the effective power behind them is decisive.

In this context, the so-called "national bourgeoisie" constitutes an ambiguous force at times. It is a recent phenomenon, originating as an offshoot of the middle class as a result of the opportunities for rapid social advancement ensuing from industrialization in various Latin American countries. Even though their interests are closely bound to those of foreign enterprises, in some cases they harbor aspirations of becoming independent and establishing themselves as an economically autonomous class similar to those of the major economic powers. They may therefore produce a kind of dynamic force leading to social transformation.

In Latin America the Christian churches have constituted an alienating factor in their identification with the prevailing social order. In certain quarters of the Catholic Church (Protestant churches have not ordinarily constituted a decisive political factor), in spite of its traditional reaction against theological liberalism, there has appeared a total identification with the commitments fostering the idea of a Western Christian civilization; in this sense, it has formed a constant pressure group. One recent sign of this attitude was the formulation of a Christian ideology of change which sanctions a partial modification of structures, leaving them fundamentally unchanged. In this way, it merely echoes the neo-liberal ideology which, in turn, is an attempt to protect privileges acquired under liberalism in the face of the pressure of new socio-economic circumstances.

Despite their middle-class—and to some extent lower-class—extraction, the armed forces have become the custodians and arbiters of the established order, if not its principal protagonists. Nevertheless, in certain areas a new nationalist trend has led them to a more critical stance toward the most flagrant manifestations of influence by foreign pressure groups, but this is partially neutralized by their extreme fear of everything they regard as communist. And it is as such that all the renewal forces are presented to them in incessant propaganda. In addition, their isolation from other social sectors and the continual ideological indoctrination to which they are subjected deprive them of the necessary sensitivity to empathize with the people's cries for social justice.

The labor force, unforeseen in the liberal order, is a crucial factor in the development of political consciousness and could well constitute a fitting instrument for the realization of the aspirations of the armed forces. At present, however, they have not achieved sufficient cohesion to act effectively. Certain exceptional cases demonstrate the power of a labor force united behind coherent goals, but even in these cases there is a certain conformist tendency which seeks only immediate, limited goals within the existing social order rather than using its potential to press for profound structural changes. As labor unions are found principally in the urban centers, they fail to reach the peasant masses which still comprise the bulk of the Latin American population.

With the exception of the rise of the industrial bourgeoisie and some rudimental labor organizations, the picture is not, after all, new. What then justifies our speaking of a crisis in the Latin American political structures? While the lack of any visible correspondence between the formal theory of the decision-making process and the actual reality may be a crucial condition, it is not sufficient proof of a state of crisis.

In our continent there has always existed a popular majority lacking any real share of power because of lack of access to the decision-making which affects their own destiny. The condition of these masses is quite distinct from that in highly developed nations in which the marginality of the masses is not absolute, since they are generally granted at least formal participation. Moreover, because the major economic nations benefit also from a large portion of the wealth of the underdeveloped nations, the wealth amassed is sufficient for their governments to be able to raise the general standard of living to such a point that violent outbreaks are avoided and their frustrations are kept from materializing in the political field.

In contrast, in our continent broad sectors of the population, in some cases comprising a majority, have absolutely no share in political affairs, not even formally. In addition to the actual political proscriptions their own ignorance, a result of their poverty, prevents them from using the few political means theoretically at their disposal (for example, the vote). We are told that "men are free to make history"; but "certain men are freer than others," since such freedom presupposes satisfaction of the essential needs of food, clothing, and shelter. In Latin America only a very small minority possess these in satisfactory form. The men, restricted from the creative processes of their nation and reduced to mere instruments of production for other men, not only do not make history; they are like objects, unable to determine their own lives. Events pass them by; they have no control of the processes in which they are involved.

With the advance of technology, however, the outcasts of our society have acquired a subjective consciousness of their wretchedness, which they formerly accepted as a "natural" necessity. Through mass media which reach even the illiterate with image and sound, they have suddenly discovered that their living conditions are not "necessary" to world order or to any preestablished natural order. Suddenly they have criteria for comparison which have broken for good their fatalistic attitude of silent suffering. One of the outward signs of this new state of affairs is the rise of great internal, and even international, migrations of the peasant sectors.

The marginal sectors have begun to develop a political consciousness and to feel the need to really share in the decisions affecting them. In the present Latin American political structure, however, there are no channels through which the masses can satisfy their growing demands. The liberal order has allocated power to a few to the benefit of a minority. The aggregate of liberal values has no vital and functional relation to life and to the needs of the vast mass of society.

The revolutionary context involves the following changes: power seizure by a group or groups disputing the validity of the prevailing system; radical changes in the economic, political, social, and cultural structures; establishment and consolidation of a new institutional order. Although revolutions appear to erupt without warning, they in fact climax a preparatory phase which consists of realizing the urgent need for these changes. The legal justifications of the existing power begin to take on negative connotations, and a whole new array of values appears on the scene.

One must not confuse "revolution" with other processes such as "reform" (which occurs within the existing institutional framework) and "development." There can be development which does not lead to revolution, and vice versa. Development occurs when all the human factors in society come to life and unite in a common creative endeavor. And a change of administrations, no matter how violent, without structural change is only a *coup d'état*, a palace revolt, etc.

Within Latin America revolutions have occurred in Mexico, Bolivia, and Cuba. In Cuba a revolutionary process fitting the given technical definition continues even now. In the other two cases there has been a definite stagnation of the process of change, leaving projected goals only partially realized; they are sometimes classified as "abortive revolutions."

In the course of this study we have noted the existence of major sectors in our continent with no real share of power, who are now conscious of this fact and aspire to an active participation in the events that determine their own destinies and those of their nations.

Our analysis of the apparatus designed by the established order for the participation of the people in the power process has demonstrated its impotence for satisfying popular interests. Such is likewise the case with the political parties which should constitute the natural and principal structure within the liberal regime to channel the interests of different social groups but which lack the vitality necessary for rapid social change today. Their main goal is election, an attitude which in the present situation constitutes an evasion of responsibility. It is becoming increasingly doubtful whether social changes can be effected within the established political order; the wooing of the masses is done only with demagogic and electoral ends, producing no real mobilization of the people. Moreover, the hardening of conservative positions has a repressive and even prohibitive effect on the progressive movements even in the electoral contest. When, at best, some of them attain power to carry out minimal basic reforms, they run up against the pressure of reactionary forces which operate in two ways: by forcing them to compromise, thus rendering them ineffectual, or by divesting them of power.

The inability of the liberal political institutions to respond creatively to the revolutionary changes of our times and to cries for social justice is a dangerous obstacle to popular aspirations. The marginal sectors have therefore begun to suspect that seizure of power, by whatever means, is the only way to succeed in initiating the changes necessary for the integration of a truly human community.

There are also other factors which justify speaking of a "revolutionary situation." A large portion of the "middle class" has begun to realize that they also belong to the politically marginal sector, because their political participation is an illusion and because they have been until now unwitting tools in the defense of a status quo not in accord with their personal aspirations. This realization, together with a genuine ethical concern, has led individuals from the professional, intellectual, and middle classes to ally themselves voluntarily with the groups of greatest suffering.

The composition, methods, and efficacy of these groups vary greatly from place to place. As indicated, university students, intellectuals, and professionals are the habitual forces. Nevertheless, recent events reveal an extension of this attitude to sectors traditionally bent on defending the status quo: the religious (Camilo Torres in Colombia), the military (Francisco Caamaño Deñó in the Dominican Republic), the professional and traditional upper-class (Fidel Castro and Ernesto Ché Guevara, Cuba and Argentina-Cuba).

The methods vary tremendously from region to region: open and latent guerrilla activities (Peru, Venezuela, Guatemala), the struggle of the indigenous Indian population (Colombia), and an insensible lethargy distinguishing certain regions (Argentina).

The failure of the revolutionary leadership in some cases is a result not only of the alienation of the popular sectors but also of the sterile isolation of the Latin American professional and intellectual. They blindly imitate foreign patterns and diffuse only the bookish elements which exert no influence on the actual environment. This fastidious elitism is deliberately encouraged by the "powers that be" to impede the possibility of true human contact with the suffering masses.

One may only speculate as to how, when, and at what points Latin America will realize the revolutionary changes which it requires as an integral part of that vast mass of humanity comprising the "poor nations," or "third world." One thing is clear, however: Individuals and groups must become conscious of the present injustice and its profound roots and prepare themselves not only to participate in and direct the action but to involve others in it. The greater the participation of the governing, teaching, and technical groups in the revolutionary process, the less will be the social cost and the use of violence in the revolution, the more rapid will be the transition to new institutions, and the more effective they will be. This statement is valid regardless of which ideology finally determines the direction of the revolutionary forces.

Revolution is not, then, a natural force or fate. It is a goal-oriented process generated by men for men, so we must ask ourselves, What is the ultimate purpose of revolution in our particular situation? As general, tentative suggestions we note the following needs: to improve Latin American man's standard of living; to seek a thorough "humanization"; to promote full access of the people to political and economic power; to seek new and more authentic forms of community life; to fashion ways of advancing the responsible awakening of the people to the historical process in which their country is living and means of appraising creatively their own cultural forms within a well-founded universal frame of reference; to avoid the danger of a centralizing bureaucracy by promoting popular responsibility for and management of intermediate organizations such as neighborhood associations, councils, cooperatives, etc.

On the other hand the structural crisis in Latin America could also foretoken a strengthening of the status quo by counterrevolutionary means and the subsequent direct seizure of power by reactionary groups. The counterrevolutionists would come from the traditional groups of the nation interested in the established order, in spite of the inherent contradictions in that order. They would act at the instigation, if not under the forthright direction, of extracontinental, ostensibly international groups under the cover of institutions whose goal is to protect lucrative markets for investment and sources of crucial raw materials. These institutions appear as diplomatic corps, hemispheric or international institutions for economic "aid," and even as continental police forces defending "ideological boundaries."

In this context each study should be careful to avoid a narrow unenlightened localism. Together in the total effort they should come to grips with hemispheric and worldwide problems. For "peaceful coexistence" for some means freezing a wretched economic status for others.

Neither should one ignore the possible importance of struggles beginning to break out in the economically sound nations from sources similar to those of Latin America. Such, for example, are the complex current events which compose a potentially revolutionary situation in the United States. The evolution of technology has introduced even in the economic powers of traditional capitalist standing new factors threatening the relatively high standard of living of the general population. The uprising of the U. S. Negro aspiring to become a citizen with full rights is another significant event. In the United States there are signs that such real structural change has now reached the level of a conscious process: the struggle for racial integration; the consciousness gained by a large portion of the U. S. population of their relatively low economic status; the open signs of solidarity with those fighting for their freedom and autonomy in Vietnam and the Dominican Republic; the new generation of students and intellectuals who identify with the suffering people. This last fact offers us a new generation who can talk with us in the vital context of similar concerns and ends, not in a paternalistic fashion.

Finally, we must point up the difficulties confronting a peaceful, constitutional process of structural change, although certain situations (as in the Chilean case) force us to suspend final judgment. Every responsible man must face the question of the "social cost" of a violent revolution. A penetrating study of the problem is urgently needed; the absence of serious inquiry concerning the unqualified affirmation of "pacifism" constitutes an evasion of one of the burning pertinent issues.

The Bible conceives a highly dynamic relationship between God and man as reflected throughout the scriptures in the tension between God's redemptive purpose beginning with the creation and man's constant rebellion against it. This dynamic is seen in the fact that God himself destroys the institutions which he has ordained when they usurp his own position (the Kingdom in Israel). The same tension appears in the formative years of the Christian church as recorded in the simultaneous affirmations, "Let every person be subject to the governing authorities" (Rom. 13:1) and "We must obey God rather than men" (Acts 5:29).

Each example of this dynamic relationship in which God gives and takes away, revises and revokes, presents a new judgment and a new call to man and to the people of God. Man, the believer in Jesus Christ, thus learns to live in the present with his hope in the future which God will bring to pass. In Jesus Christ God reveals his will to act in history, to work through historical changes and movements toward a preestablished final goal. And so even as God awaits man's response, man is called to be faithful in spite of his constant infidelity; to go about working out his salvation with "fear and trembling" because the "will as well as the act" are from God; to live in diaspora (dispersion, insecurity) far from the promised land, the ark, and the altar, for "I am with you always, to the close of the age" (Matt. 28:20)—that is, to the end of time and to the ends of the earth.

This is a good opportunity to ask whether this basic fact to which the scriptures testify is not the clue for the individual Christian and the entire church to understand the present existential circumstances in which they live and act. The Christian church finds itself, as a result of God's own transforming action, in a new diaspora similar to that of Israel and the early Church; and so, just as they did in that time, we must learn to live amid secular realities.

The Christian community of Latin America today finds itself in the midst of crisis and revolution of the political structures throughout the continent, immersed in a process that conditions its way of life and forms of organization, whether or not it either wills or recognizes the fact. But on finding itself thus within the process, the church cannot therefore hope to give a specifically "Christian" impulse to this change or revolution. Such an attempt would mean sacralizing the revolution, a temptation against which God continually warns us by reminding his church in every historical situation: "I am the LORD your God . . ."

With this end, "to present every man mature in Christ" (Col. 1:28), that is, in order for Jesus Christ to become incarnate in the new interdependent society, the Christian must vitally integrate himself into the situations and communities that constitute his historic context. This integration implies no alternative or challenge to the lordship of Jesus Christ but rather a real, full, and loyal involvement in secular concerns and in the imperative decisions necessitated by the contemporary crisis. In these terms there are no grounds for the church to project a form of change or revolution which it considers distinctly "Christian" or to try to impose that same stamp on a particular social order or specific political movement. On the contrary, participation in political life and social change impels the church to assume the role of the suffering servant, to act in self-renunciation and humility for the well-being of man. On the basis of this concept we may note certain lines of action and possible responses to various anxieties of Christian individuals and churches in Latin America.

Political participation leads the Christian to responsible and creative action within the existing political parties and civic and social movements. If these do not satisfy the expressed need for social changes, he may consider joining other men similarly concerned and dissatisfied with the status quo in seeking new structures or political movements through which to direct themselves in responsible action. But he should avoid the temptation to think in terms of "Christian" political parties, which misconstrues the true foundations of the unity of the church and leads to sanctioning a particular political program with a presumed sys-

tem of Christian values (cf. the report of the Huampaní
Conference, *Encounter and Challenge*, pp. 43 f.). On the
other hand he should not be afraid to participate in groups
or movements whose politico-social concepts seem implicitly
or explicitly incompatible with the "Christian" concept of
the social system. In the first place it is doubtful whether
there exists a static and definitive biblical concept of society,
so all the systems which have been called "Christian" over
the years have been in fact historical and therefore transitory expressions of social order, no matter how biblically
inspired they may have been. Second, it is precisely within
the groups and movements questioning the place of the
Christian faith that the believer in Jesus Christ can attain
his truly prophetic dimension and embody the presence of
his Lord in the midst of the crucial decisions of contemporary society. One must recognize the danger inherent in
such involvement, but at the same time, one must not fail
to recognize also that the Word of God urges such a stand
and that in such a way the Christian's faith and his calling
to witness and service acquire concrete content.

Can the Christian participate directly in the struggle
against the established legal structures when there is no
prospect that these will be transformed through the actions
of existing political movements and parties or social pressure
groups? In other words, is it lawful for the Christian actively
to participate in revolutionary movements that may resort
to violence in cases where the goal of social transformation
does not appear viable by any other means but which is
indispensable from the viewpoint of social justice and human
well-being?

A realistic consideration of this problem should bring
one to realize that it is not a matter of introducing violence
into a society without violence. There exists the so-called
"invisible violence," or "white violence," and also moral

violence, daily latent and ineradicable from our society at the present moment. This already-existent violence results at every moment in hundreds of deaths from hunger, poverty and disease in Latin America and deprives the man of our continent of the basic necessities for living under "human" conditions. This is to say that the legal social order prevents a man from fulfilling the purpose for which he was created, that of reaching human fullness, the true measure of Jesus Christ.

On the other hand it is necessary to underscore the ambiguous character of all action, violent or nonviolent; whether we choose the way of violence for the sake of effectiveness or whether we choose nonviolence in order to preserve our principles, we are equally under the judgment of God. Neither violence nor nonviolence, therefore, can be settled in advance in virtue of a priori principles without consideration of the given situations. In the face of this ambivalence, the unequivocal responsibility of the Christian is to point out and unmask all forms of visible or invisible violence, to seek its causes and possible remedies, and to put into practice the solutions which he believes to have found in the light of the Word of God—knowing that the very realism of the Bible leads him to channel his action through existing political and social means and social pressure groups and therefore that his action can be neither perfect nor ideal.

Finally one must realize that the Christian cannot expect absolute, definitive certainty concerning the character of his decisions. This will lead him to seek the fellowship of the Christian congregation and to adopt an attitude of humility and dialogue with his brothers who have made different decisions. This will reveal to him the profound depth in which human encounter takes place in Jesus Christ, deeper even than the level of concrete decisions which of necessity we make in social living. In the same fashion as Luther, he will submit himself to the judgment of God and rely on his pardon with the words, "Here I stand . . . So help me God."

At this point one may note that there is no sure criterion for distinguishing between the action of individual Christians and the action of the church as a formal institution. Nevertheless, in certain instances the action of the institutional church must be considered as such. When the politico-social situation comes to express the demonical character of institutions and the ambition and egotism of man and when violence, direct and indirect, is unleashed in apocalyptical form, the church can and should speak out prophetically, pronouncing the judgment of God on the political parties, the economic systems, the ideologies and the governments responsible for that situation. It should indeed remember at all times that it is passing judgment in the name of the Lord also on those Christians who are actively involved in the process and that that judgment falls accordingly on the church itself. As an integral and inseparable part of the social order, the church bears the burden of collective guilt, and its judgment is always, at the same time, a confession of sin. In any case the prophetic stance implies a risk and a sacrifice on the part of the church, and nothing could be more foreign to the spirit of Jesus Christ than the assumption of a comfortable neutrality or otherworldliness indifferent to the social conflict erupting round about.

Undoubtedly the most important immediate task of the church is educational. But within the context of diaspora this effort should be directed equally toward members of the Christian community and toward nonbelievers. Calvin insisted that Christian responsibility before God is not only personal but collective; the Christian must respond to God from within the community together with his brothers.

Knowing that political activity always entails the struggle for power, the church should educate its members regarding the social and political situation in which they are involved. It should share its knowledge and its political and theological interpretation of the current situation and prevailing ideologies with individuals and political groups commonly concerned over the present injustice and searching for ways to change the order of things. Toward this end the church should constantly promote study of other ideologies and systems offering different interpretations of the process and different social concepts. For their part, church-affiliated institutions such as seminaries, study centers, institutes, etc., should try to educate those within their reach toward a greater understanding of the situation in preparation for a creative dialogue among themselves and in promotion of a fruitful encounter with the political and ideological movements of their environment. In this endeavor, which may be carried out by various means, the church should keep in mind the indispensable task of working in interconfessional teams and of promoting encounter between Christians and non-Christians. It should unreservedly share its resources and facilities and should join forces with secular bodies carrying out similar projects of study and investigation. It should make available the necessary means and prepare persons to carry out this task, and finally it should disseminate the results through all levels of its congregational life. The church must be vigilant to orient and promote new forms of parochial and ecclesiastical life which will arise spontaneously in the new situation, taking care not to preconceive a model divorced from the concrete necessities of community life and participation in the social process.

In certain circumstances this educational function, which is highly pastoral in nature, should be directed toward the whole society. When clear and unanimous decisions or value judgments regarding current political events arise from within the church proper, it must speak out before the governors and the governed. It should not attempt to offer final answers; rather it should mark the limiting factors which in its opinion circumscribe and qualify the possible alternatives, point out the good and bad features of the decisions made, and emphasize the inherent imperfection of these decisions before the Lord, who represents the supreme good.

8

Toward the Meeting of Protestantism and Latin American Culture

Historical and Anthropological Aspects

The relatively recent studies of Church and Society in Latin America have brought new understandings of relationships among the churches and of their relationship to society, or the so-called secular culture. In the period in which these studies were being made, ecumenical progress was most rapid and fruitful, and a rapprochement or dialogue between Christians and sociologists or other specialists became frequent, almost normal in certain circles. Such experiences, unknown among us until recently, started to become an integral part of the life and structure of the Latin American churches.

Such a statement is obviously very broad and subject to all the risks of generalizations. We know that in spite of the nature of the concerns of Church and Society, its work, which has been accomplished through official ecclesiastical bodies, has been hindered or prevented, whether owing to the very institution of which it is a part or owing to its rather difficult penetration in certain spheres of the church. The local congregational structure and the business of evangelization, for example, seem inaccessible to everything which Church and Society represents in the line of renewal. Furthermore, it appears that this situation will not

This chapter is based on preliminary work of Valdo Cesar and on the report of the commission on "Indigenous Culture and Forms of Christian Life."

substantially change as long as we fail to take seriously the real character of our people, their culture, and their way of life.

This problem does not only pertain to programs like those of Church and Society; we have used it simply to illustrate a fact that involves all aspects of church life in Latin America. The liturgy, hymns, worship, Sunday school lessons, youth work, constitutions, and theology—all of these are far removed in form and content from the true, indigenous Latin American culture. How can *our* language and *our* rhythm be incorporated in worship, in liturgy, and in hymns? To what extent are the cultural traits of European and North American Protestantism incompatible with the style and character of our Latin American man?

Even though the relationship between Christian community and autochthonous culture is merely one aspect of a larger problem, some of the reasons for dealing with it in a Conference on Church and Society are worth examining. This may help us grasp and interpret one of the most serious problems of the church in Latin America: its relation to the indigenous culture.

The nature of the work of Church and Society carries it beyond theological considerations to the realm of sociology, establishing contacts with the social sciences while expanding the normal sphere of thought and action of the church and its institutions. This perspective introduces several elements which open new possibilities of relation and offer great challenges to theology and to the traditional institutions and structures. The encounter of Christian thought with economic, political, and cultural questions provokes a whole set of very contemporary and very poignant questions which may be extremely difficult to resolve except perhaps by pursuing this confrontation to even greater depths.

One of the central themes of Church and Society—for example, the matter of nationalism and the urgency of its manifestations—raises disturbing cultural issues leading the churchman to consider the question of imported forms of worship. In other words the reforms demanded by nationalism in political, economic, and cultural spheres also affect the local congregation, in which the Christian expresses his faith and his solidarity with others in a "cultural" medium.

> Each Latin American people is achieving a clear definition of its national identity. There is a new sense of the particular character and heritage of each nation as well as of the special circumstances in which each people must develop its life and culture. Consequently, there is emerging also a new sense of the importance of the development of national life and the integration of all races and classes bound up in a common destiny. Youth who come to grasp the importance of this process want somehow to join in it, to contribute to the formation of nationality through the creation of progressively more authentic forms of culture, of social and political organization, of philosophy and theology.[1]

Studies on the role of foreign missions are plentiful. Henry Kramer's famous book *The Christian Message in a Non-Christian World*, W. F. Werthein's *Indonesian Society in Transition*, and Kavalam Panikkar's *Asia and Western Dominance* are among many others that seek to interpret the real significance of the encounter between widely differing cultures. Historical documentation on Latin America is relatively rich, but there has been no specific interpretation in keeping with the confrontations of Catholicism and Protestantism with the indigenous cultural elements encountered by the colonizers. In its initial impact Protestantism had an almost prodigious success. The original Catholicism was backward and often hindered government action, as in the cases of Argentina (the literacy problem), or of Colombia and Brazil (official or semi-official religion). Accordingly, Protestant missionaries and businessmen were received in several countries as liberal and educated elements. Their confrontation with the Roman Catholic Church stimulated proselytism, and the entrance of countless denominations and missions generated a state of contention totally inconsonant with the nature of Latin America. Although varying with time and place, the chief Protestant concern was a numerical one. Later the numbers of native clergymen increased significantly (especially in Brazil), a positive and encouraging sign, although they maintained the forms established by the foreign missionaries.

After the inauguration of missionary work, several attempts were made in Brazil to create an autochthonous church. Father José Manuel da Conceicão, who was converted to Protestantism around 1860, left the missionaries and began an extraordinary venture in evangelism within the moulds which he deemed most adequate for the Brazilian temperament. This method stood in contrast to the method of foreign missionaries bent on destroying the indigenous Brazilian religious customs because they were considered superstitious and idolatrous, in spite of the fact that the first of the missionaries, Kidder, perceived that these customs manifested and sustained the existence of an uninformed, though deep and authentic faith. Once again for the first time since Feijoo and Kidder there arose the vision of a real Brazilian reformation in harmony with the national temperament and customs.

Why did this experience fail? Where might it have led us? Which are the good and bad fruits of imported evangelism? Coming from countries that had already known the gospel, how could missions establish themselves among us without the foreign trappings?

How can we overcome the present predicament in which missions still direct almost all Protestant activities and institutions in Latin America? In many cases the churches have barely attained administrative autonomy and remain in financial dependence. This, however, is only one aspect of the problem. Another is the need to discover a form of worship and structure corresponding to the dynamics of events around us. Missions came to us out of a static situation on continents where life maintained a degree of stability and where an urban mentality prevailed. In like manner, does Pentecostalism perhaps signify a way—*the* Latin American form of Protestantism? Can Pentecostalism serve as the basis for the new forms of Christian life so necessary for our continent today?

The Latin American population contains a very low percentage of foreigners.

> Latin America is a region of an almost completely native-born population, inasmuch as only 3.1 percent of a population of 156 million in 1950 were foreign. If the whole region, based on information from seventeen nations, presents such statistics, it is logical that each country would manifest the same trend. The highest percentages (4 percent) belong to Costa Rica, Panama, and Argentina; of these three, only Costa Rica depended upon a flow of immigration originating in Latin America itself (60.9 percent of Latin American origin), while immigration in the other two cases was principally European in origin, especially that of Argentina.[2]

The imposition of any foreign form amounts to a denial of the reality of these facts. We know that "Protestant culture" regards the expressions of our folklore as simple curiosities, when they potentially offer an exceedingly rich and natural form of relation and communication. If indeed the indigenous people hid their culture from the colonizer, we must learn how to discover the manifold elements of that culture—its origins, syncretisms, regional diversity, and artistic interpretations. The impact of modern technology, in spite of its standardizing or conforming effect, has not managed either to eliminate or to circumscribe the specific traits of each culture. Cultural anthropology asserts that every group adopts its own mode and style of being. Nevertheless, our Sunday school program, to take one example, is an imitation of what has been done in other parts of the world, which confirms the artificiality of its forced imposition.

Accordingly, we should learn a great deal from anthropologists and sociologists, and we should seek a scientific basis for research on the indigenous forms which the church and its institutions should adopt in Latin America. This is not simply a matter of varying the order of worship. While these innovations may be made, they do not necessarily indicate identification with expressions of national or regional culture. In essence we are speaking of a revolutionary discovery: of becoming incarnate in the indigenous culture. Without this incarnation we will probably never learn the significance of a new local congregational structure, a fact which should somehow reveal and express that encounter.

Toward a Latin American Protestantism

Indigenous culture in Latin America should be interpreted as the forms of life, thought, and expression proper to the contemporary human aggregates living there. "Forms of Christian Life," in turn, refers to the aspects of a culture which pertain to the *presence* of the Christian within the whole of life.

Christianity, as an excellent missionary movement had immediately to face the problem of acculturation at the very beginning of its history, as a result of the impact of the new faith on the cultural background and makeup of the believer. It would seem that this problem is precisely the issue debated in Acts 15 at the often-mentioned Council of Jerusalem. The decision made in that moment, when the problem imposed itself on the church in sharp, radical, and urgent form, established a normative principle of great consequence.

The militant opposition of Paul and Barnabas to the Judaizers and the decision to submit the matter to the mother church of Jerusalem for the final word display a wise approach. Much more was at stake than the mere question of circumcision. Since the close of the Old Testament period, Judaism had been in the process of developing a set of practices, concepts, and forms of life and worship designed principally to distinguish Jew from Gentile and to preserve the group identity of the Jew amidst the Diaspora. The Jews clung passionately to their group out of the necessity for identification, and proselytes gained access to the benefits of Judaism only by submitting themselves to its tradition. In speaking of the law of Moses, the Jews were referring to this collection of traditional prerequisites, including the Old Testament. The question, therefore, was not simply whether Christianity, in its expansion and consolidation, was going to make use of some forms of expression inherited from Judaism, but whether the Gentiles, in order to become Christians, must first submit themselves to Judaism.

In contemporary terms we can state the problem in the following questions: Would the early Christians allow their faith to remain permanently confined within the limits of a Jewish sect? Would they allow the new faith to do nothing more than present to the world forms of religious life already manifest in Judaism, some of which stemmed directly from an undisguised contempt for the Gentiles? Would they impose on the Gentiles those obligations which, for the most part, they resisted—an imposition which signified submission to a specific form of culture before the acceptance of a new faith?

The inspired answer of the Apostolic Council (Acts 15),

established forever the necessity in mission work of distinguishing between Christian faith and its successive and manifold acculturations. It gave the young churches the freedom to maintain the ties with their culture, to choose in accordance with their own cultural makeup the most adequate means of living and communicating the Christian faith.

When the gospel reaches a man or group of men, it affects the whole man completely and immediately calls into question the cultural values which he has acquired, triggering a crisis in which he must reevaluate the various aspects of his own culture. In the middle of the crisis the believer learns repentance and comes to understand the full meaning of his faith and calling.

An examination of existing anthropological studies has become indispensable in order that any effort to understand the place of Protestantism in the Latin American context may take into account concrete situations and different expressions of culture. From this standpoint we must examine the indigenous heritage so strong in some countries (Indians comprise 75 percent of the populations of Bolivia and Guatemala), the Spanish and Portuguese heritage, the African influence, and finally the socio-cultural significance of the Mestizo (European-Indian mixture) and of the new currents of European and Asian immigrants. In Latin America where, according to the 1950 census, only 3.1 percent of a population of 156 million were foreigners, Protestantism should seriously investigate the ways in which cultural values are affirmed through the practice of faith.

Any study of Protestant acculturation in Latin America should bear in mind the different sources and layers of culture in our hemisphere. Pre-Colombian cultural roots are more evident in some regions than in others, surviving in clear manifestations even today in Mexico, Guatemala, and the Andean regions of South America. We must inquire to what extent these cultures can and should be preserved and why certain cultural traits tend naturally to disappear.

The impact of the European cultures, Spanish and Portuguese for the most part, brought a general disdain (with few exceptions) for indigenous cultural forms and consequently their systematic subjugation corresponding to the imposition of features of the imported culture, which was predominantly religious. The independence movements opened the door to European and North American cultural influences, leading in some cases—especially among the nineteenth-century ruling elite—to servile imitation of French, English, German, or North American cultures. This fascination with foreign cultures secured the adoption of individualist concepts associated with laissez-faire economic liberalism and liberal democracy. These new influences began to undermine the relative ideological and religious unity of the Ibero-American elite, coincidentally with the advent of new political and social structures and with the first influx of Protestant missions. Finally, beginning in the second half of the nineteenth century, there was an acceleration and accentuation of cosmopolitan culture in some parts of Latin America due to the currents of European, and more recently Asian, immigration. This phase coincided with the beginnings of industrialization and urbanization in large areas of our continent. Among these immigrant movements there were Protestant groups who brought with them denominational and cultural traditions which they maintained and nourished in isolation (often in a competitive spirit); thus they established themselves in cultural and religious ghettos, increasing the existing cultural fragmentation.

These historical considerations point up the need for a

study of the present and possible future trends of these cultural currents. By the same token a thorough investigation of the significance and the contribution of indigenous cultural traits in the prominent current trend toward the "universalization" of culture is becoming indispensable.

How are these historical facts related to Latin American Protestantism? Protestantism came to Latin America inevitably clothed in certain cultural trappings of the homelands at the moment in which the continent was just entering a process of transformation produced by the corresponding economic and philosophical currents. We shall need to determine in what ways Pentecostalism is related to this acculturation. The following observations, however, do not refer to the Pentecostal movement because it is so recent and complex a phenomenon that any attempt to appraise it in the present report would be premature.

We may note that the "classical" Protestant churches tend to evaluate their work in terms of numerical or financial success, number of buildings and institutions, and social prestige. In other words, their evaluation is a quantitative analysis similar to that of a business enterprise.

At the same time, Protestantism opened up several conflicts by introducing the democratic forms of ecclesiastical government into a society in which authoritarian rule was the norm in religious matters:

First, we must note the discrepancy between the democratic theories and the paternalistic authoritarian practices of the missionary, a discrepancy which was easily accepted by the majority of believers due to the prevailing norms in Latin American society.

Second, their theoretical affirmations of democracy, simultaneous with the use of manipulative methods which contradicted that basic principle, created several paradoxes or conflicting tensions: for example, the conviction, imposed by habit, that religious truth may be reached by a majority vote.

A third conflict seemingly inherent in the missionary system arises with the emergence of an indigenous clergy; because the new leaders lack the resources and paternalistic authority which the missionary has had at his disposal, opposition to the new pastors and divisions or authority crises within the community are frequently provoked.

Latin American Protestantism has assimilated in its preaching and message a "doctrine" inherited directly from its missionary origins: the conviction that the inner transformation wrought by conversion to Jesus Christ creates repercussions in one's life resulting in an improved socioeconomic situation. Although there has been no theological formulation of this "doctrine," the prevailing consensus confirms it. The paradox in this case is that belief of this sort seems to disavow the necessity of social solidarity required by the process of national development in which the nations of Latin America find themselves engaged. The "doctrine" of personal triumph (a highly individualistic concept of "success") led the church to establish a set of institutions amounting to a Protestant "subculture," that is, an autonomous organism encysted in the national culture. In these microcosms believers tend to seek isolation and refuge as is illustrated in the case of the educational systems created by different Protestant traditions in duplication of the prevailing public system. "Doctrine" and "institution" thus reinforce each other, provoking a Protestant mentality often at odds with the Latin American environment.

Although historical and anthropological studies may verify the diversity of coexistent cultural situations in the hemisphere, this brief enumeration of certain characteristic features of Latin American Protestantism reveals the uniformity of what may be called the "Protestant subculture," a phenomenon intimately related to the isolation and aliena- tion of the Protestant community in Latin America.

Keeping in mind the situation just outlined, we may sug- gest some basic lines of renewal of Protestant life in Latin America. This need is intensified by the fact that the pro- cess of urbanization and secularization in our countries has failed to overcome the isolationist tendency of certain groups, and to integrate them into the totality of social life.

The renewal of the church is a gift bestowed upon it as it obeys its calling. True renewal is something more than a simple updating or superficial acculturation; rather, it im- plies a real insertion and ingrafting of the church in the contemporary socio-historical process encompassing it. From this graft the new forms of Christian life should emerge, for it evokes a complete freedom for conceiving new forms of life which correspond to the call to mission and which presuppose greater independence of inherited church struc- tures, history, tradition, and culture. Renewal should gener- ate new ways of communicating the gospel by the spoken and written word (preaching, new versions of the Bible, promulgation of Christian literature) and new approaches to the teaching function (Christian education).

It would be difficult to establish valid criteria for the entire continent or to generalize the practical results of this indispensable renewal of the forms of Christian living. On the other hand, we must urge research on local and re- gional endeavors in church renewal, which may in turn foster dialogue or encounter to the mutual enrichment of all in view of the diversity of perspectives. The goal of such theological-anthropological studies would be to determine the following: the impact of the gospel on different groups or sectors of Latin America; the degree of acculturation of

Protestant communities to their environments; those aspects of the Protestant tradition which promote or impede acculturation and the sources and causes of such elements; the new lines of thought, action, and expression which try to interpret and express the reality of Latin America, as exemplified in the forms of worship and community organization of the Pentecostal movement; a plan and procedure for preparing the church theologically and sociologically for its participation in the renewal process.

1. Richard Shaull in "The Nature of the Church and Its Mission in Latin America," report of the Committee on Presbyterian Cooperation for Latin America (Dec. 1963).

2. *The Social Situation of Latin America* (Río de Janeiro: Centro Latino Americano de Pesquisas em Ciencias Sociais, 1965).

5200 рв.